Have you ever wondered how doubt can ⫶ your life? In *Don't Let Doubt Take You* ⫶ own struggles with doubt, sharing raw a⫶ will resonate with anyone who has face⫶ challenges, or questioned their faith. Through his authentic approach, he offers practical tools to confront doubt head-on, helping readers rediscover hope, trust in God's goodness, and deepen connections with others.

—CRAIG GROESCHEL
FOUNDING AND SENIOR PASTOR OF LIFE.CHURCH AND
NEW YORK TIMES BESTSELLING AUTHOR

In *Don't Let Doubt Take You Out*, Todd gives us permission to wrestle with God and reminds us that doubt is a part of the faith journey. With his trademark honesty, vulnerability, and transparency, Todd invites us to take our doubts and fears to the God who sees, knows, and cares. You can trust Jesus even when you can't trace Him, because He who promised is faithful.

—CHRISTINE CAINE
FOUNDER, A21 AND PROPEL WOMEN

I've known Todd since he was in school with my own children and have witnessed him leading and helping people find God's best for their lives. This book will help you know how to confront the doubt that tries to trip you up and take you out. Todd not only shares his own personal struggle with doubt but gives each of us a plan to replace doubt and insecurity with faith and confidence.

—JACK NICKLAUS
"THE GOLDEN BEAR" GOLF LEGEND

Don't Let Doubt Take You Out not only exposes the danger of letting doubts go unchallenged but offers a clear path through the minefield of uncertainty. My friend and fellow pastor Todd Mullins knows firsthand how doubt can disrupt relationships and pull you away from God. Drawing on his own deeply personal experiences and insight into God's Word, Todd meets doubters where they are and shares practical tools to overcome doubt once and for all. This book is an invaluable resource for showing how our doubts can actually lead us to stronger faith. Highly recommended!

—CHRIS HODGES
SENIOR PASTOR, CHURCH OF THE HIGHLANDS
AUTHOR, *OUT OF THE CAVE* AND *PRAY FIRST*

I have known Todd and Julie Mullins personally for many years, and the growth they have led at Christ Fellowship has been truly amazing. I try to make all my books practical and relevant to our everyday lives. Todd's book on overcoming doubt takes that same approach. I encourage you to read it and allow God to help you overcome doubt and live a more victorious life.

—JOYCE MEYER
BIBLE TEACHER; BEST-SELLING AUTHOR; HOST,
ENJOYING EVERYDAY LIFE

Some people exude the life and love of Jesus in a way that draws you in. Pastor Todd Mullins is that kind of man. His heart for people and the wisdom with which he lives are both inspirational and encouraging. Those are some of the many reasons I recommend *Don't Let Doubt Take You Out*. Todd takes us on a personal, powerful, and scriptural journey to help us overcome self-doubt and fear. I am convinced the pages of this book are going to push you forward in your purpose and walk with God!

—EARL MCCLELLAN
SENIOR PASTOR, SHORELINE CITY CHURCH

In *Don't Let Doubt Take You Out*, Todd Mullins courageously shares his personal journey through a season of uncertainty. By addressing the tough questions about God's goodness and exploring how doubt affects our connections with others, he encourages readers to embrace vulnerability and openness. This book is a compassionate guide for anyone seeking understanding and support in their faith journey.

—CHAD VEACH
LEAD PASTOR, ZOE CHURCH

For nearly twenty years, I have had the honor of watching God use the lives of Pastors Todd and Julie Mullins to build something that would have been impossible if doubt was their counselor. In moments when playing it safe would have been the more comfortable road, Pastor Todd has chosen to silence insecurity and awaken possibility. This book is not filled with pages of advice, but it is the gift of a friend taking you by the hand and speaking right to your heart. We all have doubts that want to shrink our lives, but within these pages, you will find strength shared and insight imparted so that you can move beyond the containment of fear and embrace the adventure of faith for your future. Thank you, Pastor Todd, for leading in a way that is helping so many get back to the place of believing.

—CHARLOTTE GAMBILL
SPEAKER, AUTHOR, LEADERSHIP MENTOR, AND TEACHING PASTOR

Pastor Todd Mullins lives a life of faith and integrity. His example has made a profound impact in my life. He is touching a generation for the glory of God. The truth shared in his first book, *Don't Let Doubt Take You Out*, will equip you to face your doubts head-on with the expectation that God will not just allow you to overcome the obstacles in your life but change you in the process! Pastor Todd's vulnerability will connect with your own journey, and you'll find your heart deeply strengthened for your current season and the days to come.

—RICH WILKERSON JR.
PASTOR, VOUS CHURCH, MIAMI

DON'T LET DOUBT TAKE YOU OUT

TODD MULLINS

CHARISMA
HOUSE

Cataloging-in-Publication Data is on file with the Library of Congress.
International Standard Book Number: 978-1-63641-434-8
E-book ISBN: 978-1-63641-435-5

2 2025
Printed in the United States of America

This book is dedicated to my parents, Tom and Donna Mullins, two of the greatest people who have ever lived. Mom and Dad, you both have laid the foundation of faith that my life is built upon. Through every season of doubt you have echoed the voice of God over my life. Thank you for giving me the greatest gift a parent can ever give their child, a life lived for Jesus. I love you.

CONTENTS

FOREWORD

BY JOHN C. MAXWELL

TODD MULLINS IS a pastor with an extraordinary heart, a leader with deep conviction, and someone I have personally mentored over the past fifteen years. He is also my pastor. Through the years we've shared moments of reflection, prayer, and insight. But what always strikes me about Todd is his unwavering commitment to the people he serves and his pursuit of truth—even when that truth takes him through the valleys of doubt.

Doubt is something we all experience. It's that gnawing feeling that creeps in when we least expect it, questioning our purpose, our faith, and our direction. For many of us, doubt can be a stumbling block, something to be feared or avoided. But Todd sees it differently. He understands that doubt, when faced head-on, can be a doorway to deeper faith, greater wisdom, and more profound strength. This is not just a book about overcoming doubt; it's a guide to embracing it, wrestling with it, and ultimately allowing it to shape us into who God has called us to be.

I've watched Todd lead Christ Fellowship Church with a steady hand and a compassionate heart. His ability to connect with people, to understand their struggles, and to speak life into their situations is nothing short of remarkable. And it's from this place of deep empathy and experience that Todd has written this book. He doesn't just write about doubt; he lives with it, understands it, and most importantly has learned how to grow through it.

I believe this book will be a game changer for many of you. Todd's insights are not just theoretical; they are born out of real-life experiences, both his own and those of the countless individuals he has guided through some of life's darkest moments. He offers a unique blend of scriptural wisdom, practical advice, and personal anecdotes that will resonate with anyone who has ever questioned God or wondered if they were enough.

As you turn the pages of this book, you'll find yourself in the company of someone who knows the terrain well—someone who has walked through the valley of doubt and emerged with a stronger, more resilient faith. Todd is not just a pastor; he's a fellow traveler, a guide, and a friend. And in these pages he's extending his hand to you, inviting you to join him on a journey that promises to transform your doubts into a deeper, more unshakable trust in God.

Whether you're wrestling with doubts about your faith, your future, or your very identity, this book offers a lifeline. It's not about having all the answers; it's about learning to trust the One who does. My prayer is that as you read, you will find the courage to face your doubts and discover the incredible growth that lies on the other side.

—John C. Maxwell
New York Times Best-selling Author, Coach, and Speaker

ACKNOWLEDGMENTS

THIS BOOK WOULD not have happened without my amazing wife and best friend, Julie. Your belief in me has forever marked my life and leadership. I'm so grateful God has written you into every page of my story.

And to our son, Jefferson, thank you for letting me share your story, even as it is still being written. I am so proud of you and the way you live your life.

THE DANGER OF DOUBT

God has not given us a spirit of fear but of
power and of love and of a sound mind.
—2 TIMOTHY 1:7, NKJV

TODD, I CAN'T feel anything below my neck. I can't move my arms or feel my legs..."

My wife, Julie, was barely conscious as she lay fighting for her life on the side of a mountain. I grabbed my phone and dialed 911 as I felt fear surging through my body. Would this be the last time I would see my wife alive? This trip was supposed to be an adventure, but it turned out to be a nightmare.

It had all started a few days earlier when Julie and I traveled to go hiking together in the mountains of Colorado. It was one of our favorite places to go skiing in the winter, but we had never been there in summer, and we quickly fell in love with the place all over again. Every day as we were hiking the trails of the resort, we saw people loading bikes onto chairlifts and riding them down the mountain. It looked awesome! My appetite for adventure worked overtime to convince Julie we ought to try it. I finally wore her down, and on our very last day of the trip she agreed to give it a go.

We rented the bikes and loaded them on the chairlift

and made our way to the top. We rarely rode bikes at home in the flatlands of Florida, let alone went mountain biking, but we reasoned, *when in Rome...* We arrived at the top and found the path marked "Easiest Way Down"— just a gravel service road from the top of the mountain to the base. It was a little challenging, but we made it to the bottom in about twenty minutes. Julie thought we were finished. We accomplished what we set out to do, but since I had rented the bikes for two hours, I wanted to get my money's worth, so back up the chairlift we went.

The guy at the top pointed us in a direction that would be "slightly more challenging," but we soon found ourselves in the middle of hairpin turns through trees. It was crazy. And dangerous. So we pulled out of the trees, saw the service road we had just come down about fifty yards away, and headed in that direction. What we didn't realize was that the only way to get to the service road was across a ski run. As Julie made her way across, her bike got pointed downhill and she quickly picked up speed. I remember watching as she went racing down the hill out of control. The bike hit a rock, and she was thrown through the air and landed on her back. Still to this day I can recall the fear that swept through my body as I replay the scene in my mind.

I jumped off my bike and ran to where she had landed. She was barely conscious. She told me she couldn't feel anything from her neck down. She couldn't move her arms or feel her legs. At that moment I thought our lives had changed forever. Would Julie make it off the mountain alive that day, or would our adventure end right there?

But within the next few moments *all* the feeling came back, and she felt *everything*. Every part of her body was in excruciating pain. I found my phone and dialed 911. They dispatched the mountain patrol, but they couldn't locate us. During the summer months the vegetation and shrubs grow thick on the mountain, and we were hidden by rocks and overgrown bushes. After two hours of being stranded on the side of a mountain, they found us, put Julie on a board, placed that board on a wheelbarrow, and wheeled her to the service road, where a pickup truck was waiting. After a bumpy trip down the mountain, Julie was placed in an ambulance and rushed to Vail Hospital, where they determined she had fractured her back, broken her shoulder, collapsed a lung, and shattered five ribs.

By the time we arrived at the hospital, Julie was fighting for her life. For days the doctors worked to make sure her vital organs were functioning properly. It was a long recovery, but miraculously Julie built back her strength. Her body began to heal, and we returned home with a renewed sense of gratitude for life. Julie would tell you the only permanent loss she suffered was her sense of adventure.

You might hear that story and ask, "What were you thinking? You guys had never ridden mountain bikes before, so what made you think you could ride them down a ski mountain in Colorado?" The truth is we didn't understand the risk involved. We were unaware of how dangerous mountain biking can be. Since the accident, I have read about people who have been permanently disabled and some who even died on that same mountain in Colorado. But that day we were unaware of the dangers.

My once sky-high adventurous spirit deflated into a deep sense of hesitation and doubt. After that moment on the mountain, I began to doubt my ability to make decisions and to protect my wife. I questioned my confidence in God's promises for our future together. All it took was one jarring moment on the mountain for me to be in the grip of doubt.

While doubt doesn't have the power to cause bodily injury or death, it does have the power to crush your spirit. Destroy your dreams. Limit your life. Doubt is more dangerous than most people realize. Don't get me wrong, accidents, heartbreaks, and even the mistakes we make can teach us valuable lessons about life. They can create a healthy caution that informs our future decisions, but when our doubts and fears take over, they can cripple our spirit and keep us from living the life God intended for us to live.

Our Common Enemy

Doubt—it's our common enemy. From your earliest memories, doubt was probably there. On the first day of school. Waiting for you on the playground, a word spoken, a look given. Doubt followed you throughout middle school and high school, exposing your insecurities and causing you to compare your failures to everyone else's successes. As an adult this adversary shows up repeatedly at significant times in your life, trying to convince you that *you don't have what it takes...you're not good enough.* When seeds of doubt get planted, they often produce the fruit of insecurity, fear, and anxiety, trying to trip you up and take you out of the game—all the while convincing you that you're the only one struggling in this area. Everyone else appears so confident, so capable.

But doubt doesn't just cause us to question our

self-worth, it also seeps into our relationships. When the people closest to us let us down or disappoint us, doubt whispers in our ear causing us to question their motives or their loyalty, tempting us to withdraw and isolate ourselves. *Can I trust them? Will they hurt me again?* When we listen to this voice of doubt, it becomes a destructive force that tries to ruin our relationships and diminish the quality of our life by robbing us of the joy found in vulnerability.

But doubt's greatest damage is done in the supernatural. Doubt shouts the loudest when it comes to what we cannot see or touch or quantify logically, attempting to disrupt any connection with our Creator and causing us to walk through life disjointed from the One who holds all of life together. Doubt can disintegrate the foundations of what we believe and cause us to deconstruct our faith and walk away from our God. Knowing how to defeat doubt before it takes you out is a critical skill that each of us must learn.

Doubt Defined

Doubt, in its simplest form, is a feeling of uncertainty or lack of conviction, according to Webster's dictionary. It's a natural part of the human condition. Who among us doesn't deal with feelings of uncertainty or lack of conviction from time to time? At a very young age we learn to face uncertainty because there is so much we don't yet know. And depending on your family of origin, you may have been made to feel inadequate when those moments came up. Innocent joking can turn moments of uncertainty into lifelong insecurity.

I was blessed to grow up in a family that did not add to

my personal feelings of self-doubt. My parents spoke positive, faith-filled words over my life that would shape my future and inform me of the unique gifts God had given me. When I was feeling down on myself, my parents were the loudest voices in my life, cheering me on and calling me up. In fact, I can't remember one time when they said or did anything that caused me to doubt their love and belief in me. I realize how rare that is, and I believe it's one of the greatest gifts parents can give their children. Still, I struggled with doubt my entire life. I was good in school, had healthy friendships growing up, and even displayed some leadership gifts at a young age, yet I remember doubt was always crouching by the door. Nearby. Waiting for the opportune time to grab my attention and cause me to second-guess myself.

> Knowing how to defeat doubt before it takes you out is a critical skill that each of us must learn.

We often see people who appear to have it all together, and we assume they must never deal with doubt. They're confident. Successful. On top of their game. We believe that somehow they must be exempt from this battle we're facing. I used to believe that as well, but during my years as a pastor I have counseled wildly successful individuals, men and women who have built multimillion-dollar companies, raised amazing families, reached the top of the ladder of success—and they have shared their struggles with feelings of insecurity and personal failure. Even though they may have succeeded in one area, they could only see their failure in another. They may have held the record for winning more tournaments than any other player but feel like they're losing in their marriage. They may have built a great company and experienced tremendous success but feel like they are failing with their kids. They just don't measure up to the expectations they've put on themselves.

IF DOUBT IS THE SEED, FEAR IS THE FRUIT

Seeds of doubt produce some ugly fruit. Insecurity. Anxiety. Low self-worth. But the most common byproduct of doubt is fear. Psychologists say that fear is the most common shared emotion of the human race. Fear of the future. Fear of the unknown. Fear that someone we love will die and leave us.

There are over five hundred named phobias and countless websites dedicated to helping you identify all the fears you *could have*. There's *claustrophobia*: the fear of confined spaces. *Arachnophobia*: the fear of spiders. Who doesn't have that? Maybe you have *nomophobia*: the fear of being without your phone. And while some of these are comical, the truth is *fear can freeze you up*, causing you to miss out on the life God has for you.

One scripture that helped me break free from the fear of failure is found in Isaiah 54:2 (NIV), where God tells us to "enlarge the place of your tent, stretch your tent curtains wide, do not hold back; lengthen your cords, strengthen your stakes." When you study the Bible, you see that God is always calling us to increase, to expand, to stretch, to take on more. God doesn't want you staying where you are. He wants to do more in you and through you than you could ever imagine. Think about when the angel Gabriel came to a teenage girl in Nazareth named Mary. God was going to use her to bring His Son into the world. She had no idea all that it would require, but she had to stretch (in more ways than one) to step into her calling. Jesus called some fishermen by the Sea of Galilee to leave their boats and follow Him. They had no idea what He was really asking of them, but they had to step out of their comfort zones into their callings. They had to enlarge and stretch to experience the big life God had waiting for them.

I believe with all my heart that God wants to do more in your life than you can hope, think, or imagine, but you are going to have to make room. It's like He's saying, "I can't do everything I want to do in the space you have now. You're not thinking big enough. You're not dreaming big enough. I need you to make some room for what I want to do in you and through you." And for that to happen, you have to deal with the doubt.

Doubt is a lid on your opportunities. Feelings of insecurity will cause you not to step out and take risks, and as a result you miss out on the life God has for you to live. Self-doubt will convince you that you can't, so you don't—and doubt becomes a lid keeping you from ever reaching your full potential.

Doubt is a restraint on your relationships. It will limit how deep and meaningful your relationships will ever become. You will allow suspicion and second-guessing to become the norm, restricting and restraining intimacy and vulnerability. As a result, your relationships only go surface deep.

Doubt is a disruptor to your connection with God. Because you can't see it or touch it or prove it, doubt will attempt to discount your connection to God, causing you to question your faith and drive you further away from your Father. But when you understand what doubt is trying to do, you can deal with it before it takes you out.

But doubt is also an indicator. A warning signal. Like the light on your dashboard alerting you that your engine oil is low, or the engine is overheating, doubt indicates that something needs to be addressed. It can't be left unattended or you will end up on the side of the road in life, in your relationships, or in your relationship with God.

We can learn how to deal with doubt. All throughout God's Word we see men and women who did not let their doubt take them out. They worked through it. They modeled how to navigate times of fear, anxiety, and lack of faith.

Consider Moses. When God called him to lead the Israelites out of Egypt, Moses was filled with doubt. He questioned his abilities. He feared Pharoah and that the people of God wouldn't listen to him. In Exodus 4:10 (NASB), Moses said, "Please, Lord, I have never been eloquent....I am slow

> **Self-doubt will convince you that you can't, so you don't.**

of speech and slow of tongue." Moses' doubt could have stopped him from becoming one of the greatest leaders in history.

When David had to face Goliath, he could have let doubt take him out that day. Goliath was much larger and had all the weapons to fight the battle. David had a slingshot and a few small stones. Doubt was in the valley that day, screaming in David's ear, but he wasn't listening. He learned a secret that we will explore so we can face doubt head-on.

Or consider Esther, a slave girl in a foreign land who

ends up in the palace of a king. She risks her own life to save her people. Instead of listening to the voice of doubt ringing in her ear, she takes one step toward the king, and her courage and faith save a nation.

What did these ordinary people have that we can access today? Was it more than just putting on a brave face and running toward the giant or saying a quick prayer before confronting Pharaoh?

Although I'm not an expert, I have come a long way from that moment when I was frozen by fear on a Colorado mountain. I've learned to discern the different ways doubt will present itself and how to replace fear with faith. In the pages of this book, I will give you the tools you need to make sure doubt and fear don't forecast your future. I will show you a road map that will help you make it down the mountain safely and have fun along the way. Doubt doesn't have to be a dead end. It can actually be a doorway to deeper faith, greater courage, and more intimate relationships. I'll be with you on this journey as you discover the incredible adventure that awaits you when you trust God and don't let doubt take you out.

Part I

DOUBTING YOURSELF

Chapter 1

THE WONDER YEARS: WHEN DOUBT FIRST CAME OUT

You are what you believe yourself to be.
—Paulo Coelho

W E HAD JUST moved to a new town, Paris, Kentucky. I was so excited to say I lived in Paris! It sounded so international. I was beginning the fourth grade. Another new school. Another attempt to make friends. The first few days went great. I got to know a few students, and I liked my new teacher. But then it happened—PE class. Who came up with this idea? Stop everything in the middle of the day, go into a locker room with fifty other kids, change into shorts that are way too short, and spend the next forty minutes doing push-ups and jumping jacks and avoiding dodge balls.

I forgot to mention I wasn't the most athletic kid. My dad, being the ultimate coach, had me playing sports since kindergarten. T-ball. Little league football. They were fun; I just wasn't great at them. I also happened to struggle with my weight. That first day in PE class, standing there in gym shorts and a shirt that felt two sizes too small, one of my classmates looked at me and said, "Hey, you look like the Pillsbury Doughboy." I remember all the kids laughing. If you haven't seen the commercials or picked up a package of crescent rolls lately, I think you can figure out it wasn't the most affirming comment.

For most of us the seeds of self-doubt are sown in our childhood, during those formative years when our personalities and self-perceptions are being shaped. As children we are incredibly impressionable, and the words spoken by family members, friends, and teachers can leave lasting imprints on our hearts and minds. Careless words spoken by a parent can echo for years, planting a seed of doubt for us to deal with for decades to come.

Research highlights that children's self-esteem develops as early as age four or five. By this age children form a sense of their own worth based on feedback from their environment. Positive reinforcement helps children develop a healthy self-esteem while negative feedback can lead to self-doubt and low self-worth.[1] Children often carry the burden of these negative words into adulthood, affecting their confidence and self-perception.[2]

But the Bible told us this long before modern research existed. Proverbs 18:21 (NKJV) warns us that "death and life are in the power of the tongue." Our words are incredibly powerful. They can build up or tear down. Words can inspire faith and courage or prescribe fear and doubt. And words spoken over young, impressionable minds can have a lasting effect.

I never realized until years later how much the words of that boy in PE class stuck with me. Even after I had grown four inches and lost my baby fat, that comment about the Pillsbury Doughboy echoed in my head, causing me to think I was still overweight. Proverbs 12:18 (GW) says, "Careless words stab like a sword."

Sometimes those careless words don't come from a

bully at school but someone more significant in our lives: a parent, a teacher, a friend. And when they do, they leave a deeper mark on us. Careless remarks from parents or peers can be internalized by children as truths about themselves. These negative declarations become ingrained in a child's self-identity, leading to a lifelong struggle with self-doubt.

According to Dr. Kevin Leman, a Christian psychologist and author, children who grow up with constant criticism usually develop a fear of failure and a pervasive sense of inadequacy. Dr. Leman warns parents that they hold the keys to their children's future in the words they speak over them.[3] Further, parents actually have the power to counterbalance the negativity their children encounter in culture. As parents we have the God-given authority and responsibility to echo God's truth over our children, helping them see themselves the way God sees them and walk in their true identity.

IDENTITY CRISIS

In today's rapidly changing world, our children are facing an unprecedented identity crisis. The influences that shape their self-perception are more varied and powerful than ever before. Social media, peer pressure, and societal expectations can lead to confusion and insecurity.

"Social media platforms...showcas[e] seemingly perfect lives, flawless appearances, and ideal bodies," says clinical therapist Alyssa Acosta of Loma Linda University Behavioral Health. "This constant exposure to images of seemingly perfect individuals can lead young people to develop unrealistic expectations about their own appearance and life achievements."[4] This facade can cause children and teens to feel inadequate and question their worth, leading to an identity crisis, lowered self-esteem, and even body dysmorphia.

As parents we must be the primary voice of truth in our children's lives. Our words have the power to shape their identity and destiny. Julie and I decided early on to be the loudest voices in our son Jefferson's life. We tried to make it a daily habit to affirm his value, reminding him he was fearfully and wonderfully made in the image of God. Even though he's now an adult, we still celebrate his gifts and talents. We highlight his perseverance and determination and the kindness he shows toward others. We recognize that our job as his parents is to continually remind him of who he truly is so that no other voice could possibly be as loud as ours.

THE LASTING IMPACT OF NEGATIVE WORDS

When negative words are spoken to us at a young age, they open the door for doubt. All through our life those comments and criticisms haunt us, causing us to question ourselves and our ability. It has been found that adults who experienced verbal abuse as children were more likely to suffer from anxiety, depression, and low self-esteem, questioning their abilities and worth in both personal and professional settings.[5]

I have a friend who was constantly compared to his high-achieving older brother. Despite his own talents and accomplishments, my friend grew up feeling inadequate and incapable of meeting his parents' expectations. He always felt that he was in his brother's shadow. Words such as "Why can't you be more like your brother?" echoed in his mind long into adulthood, affecting his confidence and willingness to take risks. In college he feared rejection, so he didn't try out for team sports. When he began his career, he didn't apply for his dream job because he *knew* he wouldn't get it. I watched as self-doubt took my friend out of the game, causing him to hold back from a fear of failure.

As a pastor I have counseled hundreds of people as they work through the struggles of life. During our sessions, we often find ourselves back in their childhood, dealing with something said or done to them that they've carried their entire lives—words spoken over them that

> **Words can inspire faith and courage or prescribe fear and doubt.**

marked them and set a course for their future. What about you? Does that sound familiar? Maybe words spoken in your wonder years weren't so wonderful, and now you've been weighed down with self-doubt for decades.

REWIND, PLAY; REWIND, PLAY

Without realizing it, we replay the worst parts of our lives over and over again, particularly the hurtful words someone said or the mistakes we made. In the New Testament we read about a guy named Paul who made a lot of mistakes in his life—and his mistakes are recorded in the Bible for everyone to read. Yet in a letter to a group of Christians in Philippi he gives us the secret to moving past our past. He says, "One thing I do: forgetting what is behind and straining toward what is ahead, I press on toward the goal to win the prize for which God has called me heavenward in Christ Jesus" (Phil. 3:13–14, NIV). Paul's words provide a road map for overcoming the self-doubt many of us deal with.

Acknowledge the Past

The first step to dealing with self-doubt is acknowledging the impact of the past. We can never move past our past until we face it head-on. Taking time to recognize what led to our self-doubt—what happened in our past that causes us to fear stepping into our future—is the starting point. What events from your childhood have you been carrying with you? What words were spoken over you that you've believed and received as the truth? Take the time to identify them. Name them. (See Appendix B for help identifying the lies we believe.) Processing this with a close friend will help you identify the lies for what they are. If you experienced trauma or verbal abuse, you probably need to speak with a professional Christian counselor or therapist.

Paul's admission in Philippians 3:13 that he has "not yet taken hold of it" reflects a humility about his own ongoing journey. We too must recognize the journey we're on and the factors that contributed to our battle with self-doubt.

Forget What Is Behind

Paul admonishes us to "forget what is behind." This doesn't mean we erase memories or ignore past experiences but rather we refuse to let them define our future. It involves a deliberate decision to release past mistakes or negative words from holding us back.

Often, we drag our past mistakes around with us, reliving them over and over again. We allow our failures to become fertile ground for the seeds of self-doubt. When you replay your failures, you are fertilizing those seeds, causing self-doubt to grow like a weed.

Dr. Kevin Leman, who has helped thousands of people move beyond their past, challenges his readers to reframe negative past experiences, viewing them as opportunities for growth rather than as defining failures.[6] This requires us to reframe failure. So many of us see failure as final. A loss. A defeat. When you reframe failure, you look for the lesson. Sure, you may have failed, but what can you learn from the experience? How can you take something from the failure that will inform your future and help you win the next time?

STRAIN TOWARD WHAT IS AHEAD

Paul's focus on "straining toward what is ahead" highlights the importance of having a forward perspective. This involves setting new goals and embracing the possibilities of what the future *can be*. It requires that we envision a life not constrained by past doubts but empowered by the potential of what lies ahead, removing the lid that has kept us confined

> We can never move past our past until we face it head-on.

and reaching for the big life God has for us. It requires perseverance to press toward the goal. Overcoming self-doubt is not a onetime event but a continuous process of growth and renewal. It requires persistence and is fueled by the conviction that God has more in store for us.

Words spoken over us and experiences we've had in the early years form the way we approach life and see ourselves. If left unexamined or unattended, those experiences will hold us back, keeping us from stepping into the future God has for us. I've heard it said, "You can't go back and make a new start, but you can start right now and make a brand-new ending."[7]

The chapters in your past are already written. They can't be changed. They may include rejection, loss, failure, and pain, but those chapters don't determine how your story ends. Your story is one of courage and strength. Your story is filled with hope and a future because your story is still being written. And when you take the pen out of the hand of self-doubt and fear and put it in the hand of God, He will begin to write a new narrative filled with confidence and purpose.

WORK OUT THE DOUBT

1. What words or events from your childhood caused you to doubt yourself? Take a moment to pray and ask God to show you what is at the root of any self-doubt. Write it out.

2. What lies have you believed about yourself? And what scripture can replace the lies with the truth? (See Appendix B for what God says about you.) Take time to write out the truth from God's Word. Replace the lies with the truth.

   Lie:

   Truth:

   Lie:

   Truth:

Chapter 2

THINK ABOUT WHAT YOU THINK ABOUT

When we fix our thoughts on God, God fixes our thoughts.
—UNKNOWN

I REMEMBER THE DAY our class took a field trip to Mammoth Cave. I was so excited to skip class for a whole day and explore caves in Southern Kentucky. Mammoth Cave isn't just a cave in the side of mountain. It's the largest known cave system in the world, spanning over four hundred miles underground.

I don't remember much about the trip except the moment we were deep underground, in the belly of the cave, and the guide turned off the lights. It was completely black, no light whatsoever. I couldn't see my classmates or the teacher. I couldn't see my hand in front of my face. There was no point of reference. I didn't know which way was up or which way was down, and I couldn't see a way out.

Sometimes this happens in our thought life. We allow our thoughts to wander down a path that leads us to a dark and lonely place. We never set out to go there, but something happens that turns out the lights, and we can't find our way out. It's in those dark places that doubt seems to shout the loudest.

That day in Mammoth Cave, the lights were out for only ten or fifteen seconds. The students all started screaming, and the guide turned the lights back on. It's one thing to be in a dark cave on a school trip knowing you will be home in a few hours. It's another thing to find yourself in a dark place in your thoughts. Lost. Disoriented. Not sure how or if you'll make your way out.

Olympic-Size Doubts

As I'm writing this chapter, the 2024 Summer Olympic Games are playing on the TV in the other room. All eyes are on Simone Biles, who has become one of the most iconic figures in sports, not only for her incredible athletic achievements in gymnastics but also for her remarkable journey of mental resilience and personal growth. Biles first captured the world's attention when she competed in the 2016 Rio de Janeiro Olympics, delivering jaw-dropping performances that made her a household name, winning four gold medals and one bronze.

But her journey took an unexpected turn during the 2020 Tokyo Olympics, which were postponed due to the pandemic. Despite being one of the most anticipated athletes, Biles faced a pivotal moment when she chose to withdraw from several events, citing mental health concerns. Her decision sent shockwaves through the sports world and sparked essential conversations about the significance of mental well-being.

After taking time to heal and process with her therapist, Biles shared what happened in Tokyo. Thoughts of self-doubt, insecurity, and fear literally took her out of the game. She acknowledged the power that her thoughts had when she said, "I have to put my pride aside. I have to do what's right for me and focus on my mental health.... We have to protect our body and mind. It just sucks when you're fighting with your own head."[1]

Simone Biles did the right thing in Tokyo. Taking time to deal with her mental health and well-being was bold and courageous. Her thoughts had led her to a dark and isolated cave in her mind that she couldn't get out of. She needed someone to come alongside her to help turn the lights back on.

MESSED UP BY A MESSAGE

There's a story in the Bible about a man who also got stuck in a cave. His name is Elijah. The story takes place right after Elijah confronts King Ahab and his wife, Jezebel, and defeats the prophets of Baal. Fire comes down from heaven, consuming Elijah's sacrifice, and proves that Yahweh is the true God. It is a remarkable display of God's power. But right after this victory the story continues:

> When Ahab got home, he told Jezebel everything Elijah had done, including the way he had killed all the prophets of Baal. So Jezebel sent this message to Elijah: "May the gods strike me and even kill me if by this time tomorrow I have not killed you just as you killed them." Elijah was afraid and fled for his life. He went to Beersheba, a town in Judah, and he left his servant there. Then he went on alone into the wilderness, traveling all day. He sat down under a solitary broom tree and prayed that he might die. "I have had enough, LORD," he said. "Take my life, for I am no better than my ancestors who have already

died." Then he lay down and slept under the broom tree. But as he was sleeping, an angel touched him and told him, "Get up and eat!" He looked around and there beside his head was some bread baked on hot stones and a jar of water! So he ate and drank and lay down again.

—1 KINGS 19:1–6

I love that the angel doesn't reprimand Elijah for whining and complaining, but he simply tells him to get up and eat something. This goes to show that sometimes all you need to straighten out your thoughts is a power nap and a pizza. Tell me I'm not the only one who gets a little hangry sometimes!

"Then the angel of the LORD came again and touched him and said, 'Get up and eat some more, or the journey ahead will be too much for you.' So he got up and ate and drank, and the food gave him enough strength to travel forty days and forty nights to Mount Sinai, the mountain of God. *There he came to a cave...*" (1 Kings 19:7–9, emphasis added).

THE JOURNEY TO THE CAVE STARTED WITH A COMMENT

Many of us can relate to Elijah. Something happened. Someone said something or did something that led us to a dark and lonely place. Notice in this story Elijah's journey to the cave started with a comment: "So Jezebel sent a message to Elijah" (v. 2). Basically, she told him, "I hate you, and I'm coming after you," and that one comment got stuck in Elijah's head. It took up residence in his mind, where it took root.

You would think that the man of God who had just

defeated the 450 prophets of Baal, who confronted King Ahab and his wicked wife, and who raised a dead child back to life could handle one rude text message from Queen Jezebel. The Book of James says, "Elijah was a man just like us" (James 5:17, BSB). This also means we are just like Elijah, and like Elijah we can get messed up by one negative thought. It's amazing how one negative comment from someone at work or from a friend or family member can get stuck in our head and send us into a cave of self-doubt or frustration.

Don't forget that right before this happened, God had shown up in a spectacular display of power that completely validated Elijah in front of the whole nation. Still, this one comment from this one woman sent the prophet of God running for his life. The Bible says you and I have an enemy that's just as real

> **Elijah's journey to the cave started with a comment.**

as Jezebel. Jesus said your enemy wants to rob, kill, and destroy you. He will try to intimidate you and take you out, making you believe you're all alone and forgotten.

Jezebel's comment put Elijah in a cave. The enemy took that comment, twisted it, and magnified it—giving it more power than it really had. What comment has put you in a cave? What comment has the enemy been taunting you with, magnifying what was said to the point that it has you on the run?

FEEL DOES NOT EQUAL REAL

Later in the story Elijah complains to God, "I'm the only one that has served You faithfully....I'm the only one left."

God corrects Elijah and informs him that there are seven thousand faithful who have not bowed to Baal. Elijah may have felt as if he was alone, but he was not. This teaches us a valuable lesson: Feel does not equal real. Just because you feel something doesn't make it real. Your feelings are valid, but they're not always true. Just because you *feel* all alone doesn't mean you *are* all alone. God says He will never leave you nor forsake you; He will always be with you. Just because you *feel* as if everyone is against you doesn't mean everyone *is* against you. There may be a few people who are against you, but start counting the people that have your back and believe in you. Just because it *feels* hopeless doesn't mean it *is* hopeless.

Don't follow your feelings. Your feelings were never designed to be your leader. Elijah followed his feelings that day. He listened to the voice of fear and anxiety and ran into a dark cave. He had given up and asked God to let him die. And it all started in his mind. He was deceived by what he believed. This is what happens when we treat our feelings as if they are facts.

My natural tendency is to struggle with thoughts that lead me down the path of defeat and discouragement: "I can't do everything that's expected of me. I'm not up to the job. I feel overwhelmed." Soon the feelings of insecurity start taking over, and before I know it I find myself running to a cave. All I want to do is withdraw and binge on Netflix with a big bowl of ice cream.

Maybe you've been dealing with thoughts of anxiety. You don't know how you're going to make it as a single parent or in your new job. Maybe you're facing a financial challenge that could take you out. Or maybe you're worried about your family and you're playing out all the worst-case scenarios. Sometimes we have more faith that our worst fears will come true than we do that God will come through. So here's my challenge for you: If you can change the way you think, it will change the way you feel.

Think About What You Think About

Thinking about your thoughts isn't natural, but it is necessary. If we are going to live the victorious life God has for us, we must think about what we're thinking about. Proverbs 4:23 (GNT) warns us, "Be careful how you think; your life is shaped by your thoughts." Two truths immediately jump out of this passage.

First, *your thoughts are your choice.* There are many things in life you don't get to choose. You don't get to choose where you were born, the color of your skin, or how tall you are. But every one of us has the power to choose our own thoughts. Nobody can choose those for you. The devil can't make you dwell on anything. The people around you can't make you think certain thoughts. Only you can control you. Other people's words or behaviors can try to plant a seed of negativity or doubt, but only you get to decide what thoughts take root in your mind.

When I was a teenager, my dad shared a secret that his grandfather had shared with him. *You can't stop the birds from flying over your head, but you can stop them from building a nest in your hair.* At the time, my dad was talking to me about thoughts most teenage guys battle with, but this truth applies to all our thoughts. You can't control what happens *to* you, but you can control what happens *in* you. You can't foresee what will happen later this week, what someone might do or say to you, but you can control what it does to you. Your thoughts are your choice.

The apostle Paul tells us, "*Fix your thoughts* on what is true, and honorable, and right, and pure, and lovely, and admirable. Think about things that are excellent and worthy of praise" (Phil. 4:8, emphasis added).

Fix your thoughts. Don't let your thoughts wander. Don't allow just any thought to pass the gate of your mind. Give some thought to your thoughts. There are plenty of problems you could focus on, but Paul says to focus your thoughts on what is

> **Your feelings were never designed to be your leader.**

good, pure, and lovely. Focusing on the negative will not help you. It can only hurt you. When it comes to self-doubt, focusing on your insecurities or shortcomings will not help you move forward. It can only keep you stuck, rehearsing what happened. When you do this, you keep the pain alive. God wants to heal you and help you move past the pain, but ruminating on negative thinking keeps the wound open.

You have a choice. You get to decide which thoughts you meditate on and which ones you ignore. Only you get to decide. Your thoughts are your choice.

The second truth from Proverbs 4:23 is *your thoughts are powerful*. If your thoughts can shape your life, they're powerful. That's why Scripture warns us to be careful with them. If we don't care for our thoughts, they can destroy our life. They will determine the course of our life.

Pastor and author Craig Groeschel says, "Our lives are always moving in the direction of our strongest thoughts."[2] The thoughts we dwell on and allow to rumble around in our brains move our lives in a certain direction. Which makes you ask, "What are my strongest thoughts? What are the thoughts I'm giving the most validity to?"

When your strongest thoughts are fixed on God's faithfulness and goodness, it will cause you to run to God in times of doubt. When you remind yourself that God will

> **If you can change the way you think, it will change the way you feel.**

supply all your needs; that no weapon formed against you will prosper; that God is working all things together for your good—those thoughts build your faith, or what I like to call "GOD-fidence." This is not a confidence in yourself or your abilities but a confidence in who God is and what He can do!

But the opposite is also true. When we dwell on negative thoughts—"I always mess up," "Everything is stacked against me," "I'll never get ahead"—scientists have found that the brain releases chemicals in the body that attack our health and well-being. Research has found that when you focus on thoughts of anger, resentment, and self-hatred, over time you produce a steady flow of toxic chemicals from the brain that attack your immune system.[3]

Studies have linked chronic diseases such as heart disease, diabetes, and even some forms of cancer to toxic emotions and negative thoughts. Your mind and body are critically connected. But the great news is if your thoughts are powerful enough to make you sick, they're also powerful enough to make you healthy. The same researchers found that healthy thoughts produce healthy bodies.[4] Neuroscientists have discovered that repetitive thoughts form neural pathways. They call this neuroplasticity: when our brains change our synaptic wiring, which changes our perspective on life, which changes our life. Your thoughts are powerful.

REWRITING THE SCRIPT

The year 2020 was hard on everyone. For those who were leading companies (or churches) it was extremely difficult. Caring for a congregation and a staff of over four hundred people can weigh on anyone, but it took a toll on my wife. Julie is an achiever. She's a "three" on the Enneagram (for those who know what that is).[5] It means she has a lot of drive and determination. But coming out of 2020, she lost it. She found herself struggling daily to get out of bed to face the demands of the day. Her first thoughts when she woke up were, "You can't do this another day. You don't have what it takes. Just pull the covers over your head and stay in bed." She didn't lose her confidence in God; she lost her confidence in herself. She lost her hope.

And since our lives move in the direction of our strongest thoughts, Julie realized her first thoughts were setting the tone and direction for the rest of her day. Her thoughts were holding her hostage. She needed a new battle strategy. So she wrote out declarations that she read every morning as soon as she woke up. She even kept a few of them on note cards on her nightstand. Some of the declarations were about loving Jesus and loving me (I particularly liked what she declared about me every morning!). But the following declarations were the ones that changed her thoughts and eventually changed her life:

This day is God's gift to me.

It will be full.

Full of opportunity to add value to people.
Full of challenges that I am fully equipped to take on and gifted for.
Full of disruptions that I am graced to handle.
Full of God's goodness at every turn.
My limitation is God's opportunity. His strength is perfect, so I don't have to be.

Day by day those declarations changed her thoughts, and the new thoughts gave her the strength to move forward. Your thoughts are more powerful than you know, which is why you need to give some thought to your thoughts.

Give Some Thought to Your Thoughts

Most people never give thought to their thoughts. They never evaluate what seeds they are planting in the recesses of their mind. Take some time to inventory your thought life. What are some of the recurring thoughts you think about each day? How are negative thoughts shaping your perspective on life and on your relationships?

Maybe you need to write down some declarations and speak them out loud every day. After I saw the difference the declarations made in Julie's life, I wrote my own set of daily declarations (included in Appendix C). These have helped me take control of my thoughts before my thoughts take control of me.

Elijah did something with his thoughts that hurt him. He left them unattended. He allowed them to run free, and they took him out. He became overwhelmed with fear and doubt, and it drove him to a dark and lonely cave.

What if you took every thought captive instead of being held captive by every thought? Every thought of worry—captive. Every thought of fear—captive. Every insecure thought—captive. As you do, your life will move in a different direction, one that begins to see the promise and future God has for you.

WORK OUT THE DOUBT

1. What are the negative, recurring thought patterns that impact your mood, relationships, and/or outlook on life?

2. In Elijah's story the angel gave him a very practical solution ("get up and eat"). What are some practical things you could do this week to help set your thought life up for success?

3. If you were to write your own declarations, what truths would you need to declare over your life? See my declarations in Appendix C for examples and write out one or two declarations for your life.

Chapter 3

ANTIDOTE TO ANXIETY

Anxiety does not empty tomorrow of its
sorrows but only empties today of its strengths.
—C. H. Spurgeon

THE FIRST TIME I had a panic attack I thought I was
dying. I had never experienced anything like it before,
so I had no idea what it was or how to deal with it. It
came in the middle of the night; I had been having trouble
sleeping for weeks. We were not only in the middle of a
global pandemic but months filled with racial tension,
demonstrations, and political division. I was trying to lead
our church through these unpredictable waters and help
our community get back on their feet and move forward.
The problem was, I was stuck. Ambushed by anxiety.

What I discovered was that anxiety wasn't the problem.
It wasn't sinful or wrong. Instead, anxiety was the warning
flag, the indicator light, telling me there was something I
needed to deal with.

You don't need another book to tell you that anxiety is
at an all-time high. In recent years our world has experienced changes that have fundamentally altered the landscape of mental health, bringing issues such as anxiety to
the forefront of the conversation. The profound impact of
global events, coupled with a digital age that often blurs

the lines between reality and perception, has left many of us grappling with heightened levels of anxiety. These new pressures are stacked on top of the stress we already manage in our relationships, schools, and careers.

Anxiety, at its most basic definition, is a psychological and physiological response to stress. Something happens, and we perceive it as a threat. Our mind starts to race. We worry about what could happen next. For some, anxiety causes physical changes such as increased blood pressure and leads to panic attacks, as it did with me. Anxiety looks different on different people in different seasons.

ANXIETY UNDETECTED

Sometimes you may not even recognize that you are dealing with anxiety. The World Health Organization published a list of the symptoms and patterns of anxiety. See if any of these looks familiar:

- trouble concentrating or making decisions
- feeling irritable, tense, or restless
- heart palpitations
- sweating, trembling, or shaking
- trouble sleeping
- a sense of impending danger, panic, or doom[1]

We all may deal with these symptoms occasionally, but when they become a part of our everyday life, we are robbed of peace, joy, and health. Anxiety not only erodes our quality of life, but it fuels insecurity and kills our confidence.

Research has repeatedly shown a correlation between anxiety and self-doubt. Anxiety can skew one's perception of reality, leading to an exaggerated sense of inadequacy and a distorted self-image.[2] Anxiety magnifies the problem, leading to feelings of incompetence and despair.

While we can't eliminate every anxiety-inducing circumstance or relationship in our lives, we don't have to be held hostage by this threat another day. There is a passage of Scripture that gives us the antidote to anxiety. An antidote, by definition, is "a remedy to counteract the effects of poison" (*Merriam-Webster*). This is not a pseudo spiritual or oversimplified solution. Reversing the effects of poison takes time, discipline, and sometimes help from medical professionals, but this antidote is available to each of us.

THE MOST HIGHLIGHTED VERSE IN THE BIBLE

I didn't realize that Amazon and Kindle publish a report of the most digitally highlighted verse in the Bible. The "winner" is not what you might think. It's not John 3:16, which tells us about God's love and grace. It's not Jeremiah 29:11, which speaks of the hope and future God has for us. It is Philippians 4:6–7 (NKJV), which states, "Be anxious for nothing, but in everything by prayer and supplication, with thanksgiving, let your requests be made known to God; and the peace of God, which surpasses all understanding, will guard your hearts and minds through Christ Jesus." In this passage Paul gives us the antidote for anxiety.

He starts by telling us not to be anxious for anything.

Have you ever told someone, "It's going to be OK," even when you had no idea if it really was going to be OK? When you are flying and the plane hits turbulence, what do you do? We look for someone to tell us it's going to be OK. Julie does this every time we fly. Undoubtedly, during our flight we hit some turbulence. Immediately my wife will put the death grip on my arm and look to me to assure her that it's going to be OK, as if I have a degree in aviation and atmospheric instability. Still, I tell her everything's OK.

We often face situations in life that have no guarantee of a positive outcome—problems in our marriage or finances or health. And the truth is there's a good chance it won't be OK. But you can be OK, even when everything around you is not OK.

Don't Deny It—Deal with It

All of us deal with worry and anxiety, and it begins when we are young. Kids in school worry about who they will sit with at lunchtime or if they will get picked for a team on the playground. In high school we worry about fitting in and if we'll graduate and get into college. When we get into college we worry that we may never get *out* of college and find a job to *pay for* college. Then we get married and have children and worry if they will turn out OK. *There's so much to be worried about.* The World Mental Health Survey published a report that said Americans are the most anxious people on the planet. Of all the countries in the world, Americans spend more money on anxiety medications than anyone else.[3]

Let me pause to say that anxiety disorders are real, and

many people need to be under a doctor's care for something going on in their body or mind. I am not a medical doctor, and I'm not saying you don't need medication. In fact, the same study reported that 30 percent of people are dealing with serious anxiety disorders that require medical care, but the rest of us, the remaining 70 percent, need to deal with our anxiety by changing our outlook or habits.[4]

Notice the apostle Paul gives us the antidote. Look again at Philippians 4:6: "Be anxious for nothing." Nothing. No thing is worth losing your joy. No thing is worth losing your peace of mind. Worry about nothing. You might say, "But what about my family? My family is falling apart." Nothing. "What about my job? I might lose my job." Nothing. "What about my kids? What about my doctor's report?" Nothing. There is nothing worth worrying about.

Jesus said, "Who of you by worrying can add a single hour to his life?" (Matt. 6:27, BSB). In fact, worrying never adds to your life; it only takes *from* your life. Worry is a robber. It robs you of time. Time spent worrying can never be regained. It's gone forever. Worry also robs you of your peace. So many times the things I've worried about never happen, but I lost peace of mind and hours of sleep lying in bed worrying that they might.

In this passage Paul doesn't just tell us, "Don't worry, be happy." He doesn't give us bumper sticker theology. He's not just saying, "Don't worry. It will be OK." He actually gives us the solution for anxiety. When we're facing a serious problem, we need more than just the power of positive thinking. We need more than an attitude adjustment. We need the remedy, the path forward that will heal us from the effects of this poison.

Look again at that verse in Philippians: "Be anxious for nothing, but in everything by prayer and supplication, with thanksgiving, let your request be made known to God; and the peace of God, which surpasses all understanding, will guard your hearts and minds through Christ Jesus." Paul gives us three weapons to use when anxiety attacks. And all three weapons require you to open your mouth. All three require you to speak up.

DON'T SHUT DOWN—SPEAK UP

The first weapon is the **prayer of connection**. Prayer connects you to God. It's your spirit connecting with His Spirit. And when you pray, it forces you to take your eyes off the problem and put them on the One who can do something about your problem. Prayer connects you to both the person of God and the power of God. Yet many people are intimidated by prayer. They don't know what to pray or how to pray. And when it comes to prayer, I don't know anyone who thinks they pray enough. No, most of us work at connecting with God.

Many people don't believe they know *how* to talk to God. They question if there are certain words they must use for their prayers to work. But the truth is you don't have to work up a speech to talk to your heavenly Father. When Jefferson was younger and living at home, he never worked up a speech to tell me what he needed. He usually just yelled from across the house, "Hey Dad, can you come here?" "Hey Dad, can you help me?" "Hey Dad, I need some money." That's the same way we get to run to God—as our Father.

When Jesus taught us to pray in Matthew 6, He said,

"This, then, is how you should pray: 'Our Father in heaven, hallowed be your name'" (Matt. 6:9, NIV). He starts out with the word *Father*. The first word we must learn to pray is *Father*. Jesus could have started out the prayer with "O Eternal King" to declare God's sovereignty and rule over our lives. He could have started the prayer with "Elohim" to emphasize God's power. But instead, He starts with a term of endearment: Father.

Even that word can appear formal or distant, especially when we hear it read in the King James Version with a British accent. "Our Father which art in heaven, hallowed be thy name" (KJV). But the word Jesus would have used as He was speaking in Aramaic is *abba*. It's the term a young child would use when speaking to his dad. Abba literally translates "daddy."

Right from the beginning Jesus is teaching us that prayer is all about relationship. It's all about connecting with your heavenly Father. The purpose of prayer is not to get something from God. It's about getting to God. Being *with* Him.

The Bible has a lot to say about our relationship with God as our Father. The term *Father* is used 265 times in Scripture referring to God. I realize that just the mention of that word can bring different images to our minds. For some it's connected to great memories, a sense of security, and meaningful conversations. But for others the word *Father* can bring up feelings of rejection and insecurity. Maybe your dad wasn't there for you when you were growing up. He wasn't reliable. You need to know that your heavenly Father is an ever-present dad. Always there for you. Watching over you. Anytime you call out for Him, He shows up.

Paul says that when anxiety attacks, the first place we need to run to is our Father, Abba. I have said before that prayer needs to be our first response, not our last resort. As soon as we face a problem or need that causes anxiety, we should run to God. When I hear people say, "All we can do now is pray," I wonder, What have you been waiting for? Let's not wait until it's all we can do. Let's do that first.

The second weapon Paul gives us to fight anxiety is the **prayer of supplication**. Supplication is a word we don't use often today, but in the original language it means intense prayer; a loud shout; on your face before God. It's a desperate cry for God to intervene. "O God, help me! O God, I need You now!" You can't shout that kind of prayer while you're at work or in your cubicle—you might scare somebody.

> The first word we must learn to pray is *Father.*

This word *supplication* is the same word used to describe when Jesus was praying in the Garden of Gethsemane just hours before He faced the cross. Jesus cried out to God for help. He *supplicated* with God.

Some of us are facing problems so big we were never meant to lift them alone. *I wonder how much of what weighs you down is not yours to carry.* God wants to give you peace over your problems—and prayer and supplication carry you into His presence. When you get close to God, you get close to peace. Peace isn't just something God has. It's who He is. Jesus is the Prince of peace, the ruler of peace. Peace has a name. And when you get into His presence, He gives you Himself.

The prayer of supplication is a great prayer to pray with

others. Many times in my life when I've been weighed down with problems too heavy for me to carry alone, I've called out for a friend to help me lift the load. (I will share more in-depth about these later in the book.) At times there were problems I had prayed about for so long I couldn't pray anymore. Situations in our family or certain challenges in leading a growing church exposed my desperate need for others to help carry my burden. There is power in prayers prayed in a community of faith.

Melinda, a woman in our church, was diagnosed with cancer right before Christmas, and she was scheduled to have a mass removed. In the weeks leading up to surgery, Melinda got the women in her group praying with her, praying over her. This was something she couldn't carry alone. They cried out for God to heal her body. They specifically asked for God to cause the mass to shrink. As the doctors were preparing for the surgery, the scans came back completely clear. There was no mass or cancer at all!

There's an anointing when people come together to cry out to God and carry each other's burdens. We've been created by God to be interdependent. So the next time you're dealing with a heavy problem, some issue that's overwhelming you, instead of talking with a friend about it, pray together about it. And let their faith help you carry the load.

The third weapon Paul gives us is what I believe to be the most important weapon in our arsenal to fight anxiety: the **prayer of thanksgiving**. When you open your mouth and thank God for what He has done in your life, it immediately takes your focus off your problem and puts it on His faithfulness. When you take the time to count your blessings—all the good things God has done for you—it brings life into perspective. Yes, you might be facing a valley out in front of you, but when you remember all the other valleys God brought you through, your faith is strengthened. This gives you the power to overcome the anxiety that's knocking at the door.

The prayer of thanksgiving moves you closer to God. Psalm 100 says, "Enter his gates with thanksgiving; go into his courts with praise" (Ps. 100:4). This verse teaches us how to come into God's presence—with thanksgiving and praise. Psalm 22 tells us that "God inhabits the praises of his people" (v. 3, KJV). Every time you thank God for what He has done in your life, you are inviting His presence into your life. And His presence has the power to change any problem you're facing.

Robert is an inmate at a state prison where we hold weekly services. He had been praying that his relationship with his daughter be restored. She had not spoken with her father for over three years. Robert told our prison pastor that just weeks after asking God to heal their relationship, his daughter came to visit him for the first time. He was so grateful and excited that God had answered his prayer. Even though he still has years left on his sentence, his spirit of gratitude and his prayers of thanksgiving brought hope to his heart and changed his outlook on his situation.

To recap, here is Paul's antidote for anxiety:

- the prayer of connection
- the prayer of supplication
- the prayer of thanksgiving

When you use these three weapons against fear and doubt, Paul declares the promise you'll experience: "And the peace of God, which surpasses all understanding, will guard your hearts and your minds in Christ Jesus" (Phil. 4:7, BSB). The peace of *God*. This is not the kind of peace you get by taking an extra day off work or going on vacation. This is God's peace. It belongs to Him, and it comes from Him. He's the only one who can give it. And when He gives it, no one can take it away. God's peace is not attached to your circumstances. It is attached to the person of Christ. More than just an emotion of peace, this is God giving you the person of peace, Jesus, our Prince of peace.

> **Peace isn't just something God has. It's who He is.**

All of us will face anxiety in life. There are circumstances beyond our control that will disrupt our joy and disturb our soul. Anxiety is inevitable. But what you do when anxious thoughts come flying at you will determine whether you experience panic or God's peace. Paul's promise in this verse can be distilled to this: Turn your worries into prayers, and God promises His peace.

Every time a worry-filled thought finds its way into your mind, turn it into a prayer. If you're worried about your finances, stop and pray about your finances. Ask God for what you need. If you're worried about your kids, stop and turn that worry into a prayer. Ask God specifically what you need Him to do in your children's lives. If you're worried about your career, stop worrying and turn that worry into a prayer. What I've discovered is that every time I turn worry into a prayer, God gives me His peace.

WORK OUT THE DOUBT

1. Do you identify with any of these symptoms of anxiety?

   - trouble concentrating or making decisions
   - feeling irritable, tense, or restless
   - heart palpitations
   - sweating, trembling, or shaking
   - insomnia
   - a sense of impending danger, panic, or doom

2. First Peter 5:7 (NIV) says, "Cast all your anxiety on him because he cares for you." Write out a prayer thanking God for His care for you, and give your anxieties to Him.

Chapter 4

THE COMPARISON GAME: WHY NOBODY WINS AND HOW TO STOP PLAYING

Why are you trying so hard to fit in when you were born to stand out?

—OLIVER JAMES

I REMEMBER THE YEAR our family moved to Palm Beach County, Florida. It was the summer before I entered middle school and through some connections my father had, I received a scholarship to attend an exclusive, private school in the area. The vast majority of the students came from extremely wealthy families. We, however, came from a small town in Kentucky. Nothing wrong with Kentucky. I think back on my years there with fond memories. It's just drastically different from the world of butlers and nannies that many of my classmates grew up with.

Before moving to Florida, I didn't know any of the designer brand clothing the other students wore. I didn't even know there was such a thing as designer clothing. I thought "Husky" was a brand name since all my clothes had that on the label. Then there were the cars their parents drove to drop them off at school every day. I had never seen cars like this. One kid arrived in a stretch limousine— very different from the used orange Volkswagen my mom drove. To say there was a gap between the life they lived and the life I was living is an understatement.

As if moving to a new town and enrolling in a new school wasn't enough, it was *middle school*. Middle school years are the years where self-doubt seems to shout the loudest. One day you're a kid having fun in elementary school, and the next day you're a teenager thrown in a class with kids that look like they already have their driver's licenses.

Up till then, that year in the new private school was one of the hardest years of my life. I remember thinking, "I shouldn't be here. I don't belong. I'm not like any of these kids." I was playing the comparison game—a game I've often played without realizing it. But through the years I've learned that when you play the comparison game, nobody wins.

Comparison Leads to Doubt

Anytime we compare ourselves to others—what they have or what they've accomplished—it can only lead to feelings of inadequacy and self-doubt. We end up undervaluing the good in our lives because it doesn't seem *as good* as what others have in their lives. Comparison is more than just a harmless habit; it is a corrosive force that undermines our self-worth and distorts our perception of reality. When we measure our lives against the perceived success or happiness of others, we fail to see the unique journey God has laid out for us. Instead of celebrating our own achievements and blessings, we become fixated on what we lack.

In today's digital age the temptation to compare ourselves to others is heightened by social media. Platforms like Instagram, Facebook, and TikTok often present an idealized version of reality, where people showcase the best moments of their lives while hiding their struggles and imperfections. This constant exposure to others' highlight reels can create a false sense of reality and make us feel like we are falling short.

A study that examined the effects of social media on users' mental health found that prolonged use led to increased feelings of envy and decreased life satisfaction. Feelings of inadequacy were triggered by viewing other people's posts, because

> **Comparison is more than just a harmless habit; it is a corrosive force that undermines our self-worth.**

we tend to compare our everyday lives, with all its struggles and imperfections, to the polished, seemingly perfect lives of others we see online.[1]

Another study found that Instagram use is particularly linked to negative body image and low self-esteem, especially among young women. The visual nature of Instagram, which emphasizes appearance and lifestyle, exacerbates the tendency to compare oneself to others.[2] Seeing a constant stream of images depicting perfect bodies, luxurious lifestyles, and seemingly flawless relationships can make users feel inadequate and unhappy with their own lives. Decades before social media ever existed, President Theodore Roosevelt declared that "comparison is the thief of joy." Comparing ourselves to others will rob us of joy because it breeds a spirit of discontentment.

Learning a Secret

The apostle Paul spoke to this when he said, "I have learned how to be content with whatever I have. I know how to live on almost nothing or with everything. I have learned the secret of living in every situation, whether it is with a full stomach or empty, with plenty or little" (Phil. 4:11–12). We are not naturally a contented people. We are made with a desire to acquire. Dogs collect bones. Squirrels gather acorns. Women collect shoes. And it's not intrinsically bad, but when it gets out of control our focus gets out of focus and our priority in life becomes all about satisfying our desires.

Have you ever been around a discontented person? Never really satisfied. Nothing is quite good enough. Discontentment brings unrest to the soul. And that unrest will impact the home, the marriage, and the workplace. Comparison breeds discontentment.

But in this passage in Philippians, Paul tells us contentment can be learned. In the same way that we can learn how to read or write, we can learn how to be content. Personally, this is a lesson I have been *learning* my entire life. By nature I am a very driven person—just ask the people around me. I always think there is a better way to accomplish something. I've never managed a hotel, but every time I stay at one I have a list of things they could improve. I've never been a flight attendant or a gate agent for an airline, but I'm sure I could improve the boarding process. And while an "eye for detail" can be positioned as a positive attribute, if I'm not careful it can become a detriment, breeding a spirit of discontentment and impatience.

THREE KEYS TO UNLOCKING CONTENTMENT

1. Develop an attitude of gratitude.

The first key to learning contentment is developing an attitude of gratitude. First Thessalonians 5:16–18 (BSB) tells us, "Rejoice at all times; pray without ceasing; give thanks in every circumstance, for this is God's will for you in Christ Jesus." Paul is not telling us to give thanks *for* all the circumstances we go through. He is telling us to give thanks *in* all the circumstances we go through. It's not "Lord, thank You that I have no money in my bank account, and thank You that my car broke down today." No. It's "Lord, thank You that You are my provider, my source, and my supply. Thank You that You are my Father and You know how to take care of me. Thank You that I have a car that can even break down, because a lot of people would love to have a car!"

Many of us have trouble

> **Comparison breeds discontentment.**

with gratitude because we've developed a "when and then" mindset. When I get married, then I'll be happy. When we have kids, then we will be content. When I get that job, that car, that home, then I will finally be good. *Sometimes we get so busy trying to get more that we miss what we have.* Someone once asked billionaire Howard Hughes what it takes to make a man happy. Hughes responded, "Just a little more." I fear most people fall into that trap. Don't be one of them. Develop an attitude of gratitude.

One of the ways I've done this is to list the things in my life that I'm grateful for. I write them down. Throughout most of my life I wasn't very consistent in journaling. It seemed to take too long to write out everything I was

thinking. But in the past few years I've been more intentional to slow down, write out my prayers, and write down
the things I'm grateful for. I realized that if all I see is what
is wrong in my life, I'll never see what is right in my life.
Take time to thank God for all that is right in your life
and the list will grow.

2. Put your trust in Christ not in circumstances.

The second key to unlocking contentment is to put your
trust in Christ not in circumstances. When we read what
Paul says about learning the secret of contentment, he fin-
ishes by saying, "I can do all things through Christ who
strengthens me" (Phil 4:13, NKJV). That happens to be one
of the more misquoted verses in the Bible. It has been used
as motivational fodder to take on any problem that may
seem insurmountable, but that's not what Paul meant in
this passage.

Remember, he's talking about learning the secret of
being content, and in this context he says, "I have learned
the secret of being content....I can do all this through him
who gives me strength" (vv. 12–13, NIV). In the Greek that
sentence best translates "I can do *all this* through Christ
who strengthens me." All what? The "all this" he is referring to is learning the secret of contentment. Paul had to
learn contentment by depending on Christ, not on his
own strength or his own abilities. Not on his possessions
but on his possession of Christ in his life. That's where
true contentment is found.

When we put our trust in things of this world, we will
always come up empty. The things of this world will fail us
every time. Finances come and go. The stock market goes
up and down. Jobs come to an end. Even relationships will

fall apart. And when your hope is based on those things, when they fall apart, you fall apart too. But when your hope is in Christ, He will give a peace and contentment that the world can never give. Put your trust in Christ, not in your circumstances.

3. Live with eternity in view.

This third key to learning contentment reminds us to live as citizens of heaven—a theme that runs all throughout Philippians. In chapter 1 he tells us, "Above all, you must live as citizens of heaven..." (v. 1:27). In chapter 3 he reminds us that "our citizenship is in heaven,

> If all I see is what is wrong in my life, I'll never see what is right in my life.

and we eagerly await a Savior from there" (v. 3:20, BSB). Paul echoes what he has been writing throughout the New Testament: to fix our eyes on what is unseen. What is seen is temporary, but what is unseen is eternal.

So much of the comparison trap is based on things that are temporary. Here today, gone tomorrow. We see something our coworker has, and we feel as if something is missing in our own lives. We see the car they drive, the vacation they just took. We see the success they're experiencing, and we feel like we're failing.

CHANGE THE RULES, CHANGE THE GAME

Julie and I were youth pastors right out of college. Every summer we would take our students to a Christian camp for churches from all across the United States. There were all the typical camp activities, with one caveat. They would divide us up into teams to compete all week long, and the team with the most points at the end of the week won. I'm not sure what the prize was, but it didn't matter. We had to win. I forgot to mention that Julie and I are extremely competitive, so we took our assignment seriously. We even had our team practicing during the camp's "free time." I know.

The first few days we were dominating. I think we won nearly every event. The judges gave points for team spirit, so we created a cheer and lined up in formation. Each night at dinner they would announce the leader board, and every night we came out on top. Then about halfway through the week the judges announced that they were adding in points for sportsmanlike conduct. What? You mean we have to be nice to the other teams?

They changed the rules, and it changed the game. We had to start giving more attention to being kind and respectful to the other teams. We found ourselves cheering for the other teams (partly because we wanted to get those points!). Our team still won the entire camp competition that year, but we did it with a much better attitude. There's a better way to play the comparison game.

While I said earlier that no one wins at the comparison game, when kept in check, comparison can have some positive side effects. It can motivate us to improve. We see an area where someone else is excelling, and it inspires us. We gain insights and perspectives that make us better.

When I hear a great communicator such as John Maxwell or Craig Groeschel, I can study their skill of communicating and how they connect with people and allow their expertise to challenge me. Grow me. Expand my skill set. That's turning our natural tendency to compare on its head. Same game, different rules.

GET A COACH, WIN THE GAME

I remember when Julie and I first stepped into leading our church, Christ Fellowship. We had been on staff for over twenty years serving my parents' vision as they built the church, but this was different. Now we were leading. I remember comparing myself to my dad. Tom Mullins truly is one of the greatest men that has ever lived—full of integrity and character. He has a way of connecting with anyone from Uber drivers to presidents of nations. He can preach, lead, and solve complicated problems without even breaking a sweat. And I had to follow *in his footsteps*.

In addition to that, as I was beginning to preach regularly, John Maxwell was often seated on the front row listening to me. Talk about being intimidated. John and his wife, Margaret, had moved down to Florida, and John had joined our teaching team. For some reason, during the season I was stepping in to preach, he was home...a lot.

I felt myself constantly comparing my preaching to John's or my dad's. I would watch other pastors online and think, "They preach so much better than I do. I can't do this!" Comparison wasn't helping me get better; it was stirring up feelings of insecurity and doubt, and it was about to take me out as I was just getting started.

I remember the weekend when everything changed. I was preaching and John was on the front row taking notes. In the middle of preaching, I thought, "What could I possibly be saying that John Maxwell would want to write down?" But instead of being intimidated, I decided to go straight to John after the service and ask him for coaching. I decided to lean into the discomfort and get the most out of it. I asked one of the best communicators on the planet to help me get better. Every week that John was on the front row I would ask him the same question. And every week he coached and corrected me, helping me improve in my communication skills. I flipped comparison on its head that day and leveraged it for my good.

I've tried to transfer that lesson to other areas of my life as well. When I'm around people who have the gift of generosity, I ask them about their giving journey. What motivates them to freely give what they have? When I'm around people who have built amazing companies, instead of being intimidated because I don't understand their industry, I ask them leadership questions. What drives them? How do they come up with innovative ideas? When I'm around men in our church who are great husbands and fathers, instead of feeling insecure about how I'm doing in those areas, I get them to talk about their passion for their family—why they love being a dad. And all of it helps me grow and become a bigger person.

> When kept in check, comparison can have some positive side effects.

Rules of the Game

Since comparing ourselves to other people is an inherent part of life, I've decided to put some new rules in place when it comes to the comparison game.

- **Be self-aware**: We must acknowledge our tendency to compare ourselves with others, remembering that what we see online is not the full story. We can't allow ourselves to be intimidated by people who have accomplished more than us. We can learn from them, but we have to run our own race.

- **Set personal goals**: We need to focus on our own personal growth and achievements rather than floundering in feelings of insecurity. When we set and reach our goals, it builds a sense of accomplishment and satisfaction.

- **Limit social media**: Reducing our time on social media will lessen our exposure to the unrealistic portrayals of other people's lives. As a result, it will minimize our temptation to compare. All that time can be redirected to accomplishing our goals.

- **Cultivate gratitude**: An attitude of gratitude will shift our focus from what we don't have to what we do have, building a spirit of contentment and reducing the constant urge for more.

- **Flip the script**: Every time we feel intimidated by someone else's accomplishments, we can use it to grow. Seeking to understand what motivates them just might inspire us.

SEE YOURSELF THE WAY GOD SEES YOU

One of the greatest revelations a person can receive, apart from their revelation of Christ, is how God sees them. So many of us have an obstructed view. Our failures and self-doubt are blocking the full picture. We see our mistakes compared to everyone else's accomplishments.

God doesn't compare you with anyone else. He values you not for what you do or have accomplished but simply for who you are. You are His child. You are His masterpiece, and He has put gifts and talents inside you that you have not yet discovered. When you compare anything lacking in your life to the overwhelming, immeasurable love that God has for you, you win at the comparison game every time.

WORK OUT THE DOUBT

1. What causes you to fall into the comparison trap?

   - Physical appearance
   - Athletic ability
   - Career performance
   - Relationship status
   - Financial status
   - Other: _____

2. Identify two people who could be intimidating (because of their success or talent) and think of ways to turn *intimidation* into inspiration. Write out two questions you could ask them to help you grow.

Chapter 5

WHEN DOUBT DRIVES
YOU TO DEPENDENCY

*If you hear a voice within you say "you cannot paint," then
by all means paint, and that voice will be silenced.*
—VINCENT VAN GOGH

NEVER WANTED TO be a pastor. It's not that I had anything against pastors; it just never crossed my mind
to be one. My plan was to become a doctor. That was
my dream. But right before my high school graduation I
sensed a calling into full-time ministry. People often think
I followed my dad into ministry, but I actually made my
decision to become a pastor before Christ Fellowship ever
began. (So I like to think my dad followed me into ministry. Just kidding.)

Right out of college I started serving at our church.
Christ Fellowship was a very small church meeting in a
local elementary school back then, and I was the youth
pastor, worship leader, church janitor, and my dad's assis-
tant all at the same time. The church couldn't afford to
pay me much, but Julie was raking in the cash as a first-
grade teacher, so we were good. As the church grew, I had
to fill many different roles and responsibilities, and as a
result my leadership grew with it.

After serving my parents for more than twenty-five

years, the time came for Julie and me to step up as the senior pastors. We were both excited and scared to death all at the same time. As we neared the transition, the voice of self-doubt got louder in my head. I questioned if I was up for the challenge. By that time, Christ Fellowship was a multisite congregation with over eleven thousand people attending every week. There were hundreds of people on staff and a large budget to manage. As I mentioned, I didn't have much experience preaching to adults. I had been a youth pastor. If I failed, everyone would know. My shortcomings would literally be on a platform for people to see, every Sunday.

During that season, I spent a lot of time in prayer. I needed a word from the Lord. I brought my insecurities and doubts to God and told Him I didn't think I could do this. I wasn't strong enough to take this on. I was afraid I was going to fail. I remember the moment I heard God respond to my concerns, and it wasn't the response I was expecting. It wasn't the response I wanted. In a quiet whisper I heard Him say, "You're right. You're not strong enough. You don't have what it takes." Initially I thought God was affirming all my fears and insecurities and that I should consider a new line of work—maybe go be a doctor after all. But as I continued to listen, the Holy Spirit said, "You're not enough, but I am."

That day I realized doubt had led me to a revelation of God. Of course I couldn't do this. It was too big for me, but not too big for God. What I was stepping into was supernatural, so of course I needed His supernatural strength and wisdom. I nearly let doubt take me out of stepping into my calling. But instead, my doubt exposed my weaknesses and drove me to a greater dependency on God's strength.

FROM FARM BOY TO NATIONAL HERO

When I think of a person who almost let self-doubt take him out, it's a man in the Bible named Gideon. (And no, this isn't the guy who goes around putting Bibles in hotel rooms.) Gideon goes from a frightened farm boy to a national hero in one chapter, but he had to step out of his comfort zone and into his calling. He had to listen to the voice of God even when doubt was shouting louder.

The story takes place in the Book of Judges at one of the lowest points in Israel's history. The Israelites were being tormented by their enemies the Midianites. The Midianites would rush in like a swarm of locusts devouring crops and animals. The people of God had lost all hope.

One day the Angel of the Lord came to Gideon, who was hiding in a hole trying to thresh some wheat, scared the enemy might come and take what he had. The angel came up behind him and said, "The LORD is with you, mighty warrior" (Judg. 6:12, NIV). Gideon had to be thinking "Who are you talking to? There's no mighty warrior here." But we know God doesn't make mistakes. He didn't show up at the wrong address that day, which tells me *the way you see yourself is not the way God sees you*. God sees all the gifts and abilities He has put inside you. Often we focus on our flops, failures, and mistakes. We think, "How could God use me? I have messed up so badly." But God is not worried about how much you've messed up; He wants you to step up and become the person He's created you to be.

The angel told Gideon that God would use him to defeat the armies that had been oppressing His people for years. Gideon came up with all sorts of excuses, listing his faults and failures. But when you read the full story (which you need to if you haven't), Gideon became exactly who the angel said he would be: a mighty warrior that delivered his people from the enemy. Yet Gideon wasn't that mighty warrior when the angel found him hiding in a hole. He was shaking in his sandals. So how did this scared farmer become a brave fighter? Did he read a self-help book about overcoming doubt? Did he attend a conference to learn how to release the power within? No, Gideon learned a profound secret, something most people never understand.

> **God is not worried about how much you've messed up; He wants you to step up and become the person He's created you to be.**

THE COST OF DOUBT

Many of us are like Gideon. We're great at coming up with a list of excuses for not stepping out of the hole, and as a result we never step into the life God has waiting for us. The true cost of doubt is not just the decisions we second-guess or the opportunities we miss; it's the dreams God has planted in our hearts that we never pursue, the nudges from the Holy Spirit that we ignore because "it" seems so far out of our lane, beyond our comfort zone. But when we are consumed with our comfort, we will miss out on our calling.

Research has found that people who hold back on their

dreams and never take a risk are more likely to experience depression and anxiety. One study highlighted that when people allow doubt to dictate their actions, they settle for a life less than what they truly want, leading to a discontentment and unhappiness.[1] At some point in their lives, 70 percent of people experience what researchers call impostor syndrome, a condition in which a person doubts their accomplishments and has a consistent fear of being exposed as a fraud. This doubt keeps people from taking risks, speaking up, or stepping into leadership roles.[2]

From Improbable to Impossible

I'm sure if the term had been coined back then, Gideon would have been diagnosed with impostor syndrome, afraid that someone would find out he was just a farmer, not a mighty warrior. But Gideon learned an important lesson: Just as faith is not the absence of doubt, it's also not the absence of self-doubt. It's the choice to trust God in the middle of your doubt. Gideon knew he didn't have the strength or power to defeat the Midianites. He knew he couldn't do it on his own. But what he discovered was that he wasn't on his own.

When you fast-forward to the end of the story, God whittled Gideon's army down from 10,000 soldiers to 300 men who had to fight against 135,000 Midianite soldiers. What was highly *improbable* with 10,000 soldiers was absolutely *impossible* with 300. The truth is, until it's impossible, you don't need God. If it's possible, you can handle it yourself. Impossible is where God gets started. You might be up against something that feels impossible in your life.

Just remember, nothing is impossible with God. Gideon was not facing his enemy alone, and neither are you.

So with just three hundred men carrying a jar, a torch, and a horn, Gideon and God defeated the Midianites. God brought victory and freedom to an entire nation through a frightened farmer. But it wouldn't have happened if Gideon had listened to the voice of self-doubt. If he had let fear forecast his future, he would've still been down in that hole hiding from the enemy. There will be times in the middle of your doubt that God will call you to step out and trust Him completely. He will put you in an impossible situation that might expose your weakness, but it will also reveal His strength. Billy Graham once said, "When we come to the end of ourselves, we come to the beginning of God."[3]

THE BENEFIT OF THE DOUBT

Self-doubt is often viewed as a weakness, a flaw in our character that needs to be overcome. It's that nagging voice inside our head that questions our abilities, our decisions, and sometimes even our worth. But what if I told you that self-doubt can actually be a gift from God? What if instead of trying to silence that voice we leaned into it and allowed it to drive us closer to our Creator?

The most significant benefit of self-doubt is that it exposes our limitations. It reminds us that we are not all-powerful, all-knowing, or self-sufficient; only God is. In a culture that glorifies self-reliance and independence, self-doubt serves as a humbling reminder of our need for God. A healthy self-confidence is good, but left unchecked it can turn into arrogance and pride, causing you to think you don't need anything or anyone, especially not God. But when self-doubt is analyzed, it will cause you to be God-reliant, not leaning on your own understanding or strength.

The apostle Paul understood this. He was a very strong, accomplished leader. In his letters to the early church, you can hear his confidence coming through. But in 2 Corinthians 12:8–10 he wrote about his weaknesses and one particular struggle that he asked God to take away.

> Three different times I begged the Lord to take it away. Each time he said, "My grace is all you need. My power works best in weakness." So now I am glad to boast about my weaknesses, so that the power of Christ can work through me. That's why I take pleasure in my weaknesses.

Paul's words confront our natural tendency to hide our doubts and weaknesses. Instead of seeing self-doubt as something to be ashamed of, he saw it as an opportunity to experience God's power in a deeper way. Paul embraced his weakness and self-doubt because they forced him to rely on God's strength and not his own.

The same can be true of us. When we doubt our abilities, we are more likely to lean on God's strength. When we question our worth, we are more likely to seek our identity in Christ. When we are unsure of our path, we are more likely to seek God's guidance. Self-doubt can become a conduit through which we experience God's grace and power to a whole new level.

DOUBT THAT MAKES A DIFFERENCE

Self-doubt is natural. It's normal. Even neutral. It's our response to doubt that makes the difference. It will lead us to either insecurity and anxiety or a healthy self-evaluation. When we don't deal with doubt in a healthy way, the seeds of doubt grow into weeds of insecurity. Low self-esteem and lack of confidence become our identity. But if we see self-doubt as the "check engine" light in our car, alerting us to a problem, we can leverage it for our good.

So how can we leverage the power of self-doubt and allow it to deepen our dependence on God?

- **Confess your doubts**: There's no need to hide your doubts. God already knows you have them. He's just waiting for you to ask for His help. In Mark 9:24 (BSB), a father was asking Jesus to heal his son and cried out, "Lord, I do believe; help my unbelief!" This simple, honest prayer is a powerful example of how we can confess our doubts to God and ask for His help to overcome them. Gideon admitted his doubts openly, and it was his first step out of the hole.

- **Seek God's wisdom**: The Bible is filled with stories of individuals who faced doubt and uncertainty, and it offers wisdom and guidance for those of us who struggle with doubt. When you spend time in God's Word, you are reminded of *who God is*—of His faithfulness and power—but you're also reminded of *who you are* in Christ. You are

called, chosen, anointed, gifted. As you seek
His wisdom, the truth of God will replace
your doubts. Gideon didn't have a Bible that
day, but he listened to the words of God
spoken by the Angel of the Lord. The angel's
words helped pull him out of his doubt.

- **Surrender control**: Gideon had to surrender
control *of* his life to fulfill the purpose that
was *on* his life. He couldn't stay in control
and trust God at the same time, and neither can you. In our culture, surrender is
not a popular concept. We're taught to fight
for our rights and take what's ours. But in
God's kingdom, you find your life by losing
it, by surrendering to God and His plans.
When Gideon surrendered, he became the
mighty warrior he was meant to be.

The world tells us that strength comes from
self-confidence, power, and independence, but the gospel
presents a different truth: Strength comes from acknowledging our weakness and
depending on God's strength.
It is in our moments of self-
doubt that we are most aware
of our need for God, and it's
in those moments that His
power is most fully on display in our lives. So the next
time you find yourself wrestling with doubt, don't see it as
a weakness to be overcome but an invitation to draw closer
to God.

> It's our response to
> doubt that makes
> the difference.

WORK OUT THE DOUBT

1. The way you see yourself is not how God sees you. Write three truths that God sees in you. (Use Appendix A and Appendix B for help.)

   In Christ, I am...

   In Christ, I am...

   In Christ, I am...

2. Are you a natural dreamer and risk taker, or do you find yourself staying in your comfort zone and resisting nudges from the Holy Spirit? What are some ways God is calling you out of your comfort zone?

 # Part II

DOUBTING
GOD

Chapter 6

WHEN DOUBT CAME KNOCKING AT MY DOOR

*Doubt often sneaks in through a door
you didn't know you left open.*
—UNKNOWN

WHEN MY WIFE and I got married, we knew we wanted to have a lot of kids. Julie came from a large Catholic family and wanted five boys. She grew up playing basketball, and I think she wanted her own team. But when we decided it was time to start our family, we discovered that our path to pregnancy would not be as easy as we thought.

Our seven-year infertility journey caught us by surprise, as this was not an issue on either side of our families. Doctors could not tell us why we weren't getting pregnant, and when we did, they couldn't tell us why we couldn't *stay* pregnant. Anyone who has struggled with infertility knows it can be a very emotional season. Our season lasted for seven long years.

Seven years of praying. Seven years of seemingly unanswered prayers. Seven years of questioning God. We claimed all the promises and asked everyone we knew to pray with us, but still nothing seemed to change.

But after seven years, our baby boy arrived. October 24,

1995, was the day that changed my life forever. They say *if you know you know,* but I didn't know. I had no idea that kind of love was locked up in my heart. That day in the hospital, as I held this little boy we had prayed and fasted for across seven years, I had two revelations.

First, I never knew my parents loved me *this* much. I was blown away. I always knew they loved me. They never said or did anything that would ever make me question their love, but I had no idea they loved me this much. Second, I heard the whisper of God say, "Todd, what you're feeling for your son is just a fraction of what I feel for you." I remember holding Jefferson in that hospital room and weeping. Julie knew I would be emotional, but this was a bit over-the-top. I never doubted God's love, but I also never thought He could love me so completely.

Revelations and Answered Prayers

There are moments when God pulls back the curtain and gives you a glimpse of reality. Not the reality we see around us with our eyes but the greater reality of God, of His everlasting reality. The Bible tells us that "what is seen is temporary, but what is unseen is eternal (2 Cor. 4:18, NIV). That day when I was holding Jefferson and God pulled back the curtain on the expanse of His love for me, I was unprepared. Even though I had grown up in church, had a degree in theology, and was a pastor, I didn't fully grasp the greatness of His love. It shook my faith and understanding of God in the best possible way.

I realized in that moment that Jefferson wasn't doing anything to *make* me love him. He wasn't cooing or smiling or contributing to our family at all. In fact, he had already cost us tens of thousands of dollars, and he wasn't even a day old. That should have told me something. No, he was just lying there in my arms, asleep, drooling. But it didn't matter. I didn't need him to *do anything* to make me love him. He was my son. My love for him had absolutely nothing to do with what he was doing or could do for me. It was all about the relationship. And there was nothing he could ever do that would change that.

And God whispered in my ear at that moment, "This is just a fraction of My love for you." I thought I understood grace. I knew my salvation wasn't based on anything I had to do for God but only on what Jesus had already done for me on the cross—yet I had no idea His love for me was this intense and all-consuming. My response or attitude toward God doesn't affect His love for me—or for you. He loves us more than we know.

I have discovered that when God reveals something to you, it's not just for that moment in time. Yes, it can bring encouragement and hope when you're facing a problem, but a revelation from God is eternal because God is eternal. Not only can you carry it with you into your future, you *must* carry it. This kind of revelation is a gift to be unpacked over time. It is meant to be a Northern Star, helping you find your way back to truth. I once heard someone say, "Don't forget in the dark what God showed you in the light." There are times that will be dark, and you need to remember what God showed you in the light, when He pulled back the curtain and gave you a glimpse of His greater reality.

The Day the Lights Went Out

Jefferson grew up as a much-loved child. So many people in our church had prayed for us to get pregnant that it seemed as if he belonged to our entire church family, which meant we had plenty of free babysitters lined up. But when Jefferson was about two years old, he stopped reaching some of his developmental milestones. He didn't have many words and seemed a bit disconnected from other kids his age. At first I tried to play it down. He's just a boy. He'll grow into it. But Julie knew there was something wrong.

The next several months were filled with doctors' appointments, trips to specialists, and endless tests. After a few weeks Jefferson was given the diagnosis we feared the most. Even to this day, over two decades later, it's challenging for me to write the words. The doctors told us that Jefferson was on the autism spectrum. Julie and I were heartbroken. This label could not describe our son; only God could do that. Jefferson was called, chosen, anointed. That's who Jefferson is. That's his identity. But we could not ignore the diagnosis and just go on in blind faith, ignoring the facts. Although autism did not *describe* our son, it did *prescribe* a journey we would go on as a family—a journey that would include hundreds of hours of therapy every month and alter our lives forever.

> A revelation from God is eternal because God is eternal.

At that time, we didn't know much about autism. Our picture of this developmental disorder was limited to the most severe cases we had seen. The picture we had did not match the child we loved. What we came to discover is that autism is a spectrum disorder that ranges from severe to moderate to mild symptoms. Regardless, we were devastated.

We sat there in the doctor's office in complete shock. How could this be happening to our perfect little boy? He was God's gift to us after seven years of infertility. He was our promise from God. Our promise couldn't end like this. This wasn't going to be Jefferson's story.

After a few days the shock wore off and I was ready to fight. If you're a parent, you know there's something different about the desperation you feel when your child is sick or in danger. You pray in a way you've never prayed before. I remember the weeks after receiving the diagnosis: My faith was strong. We had seen God perform miracles in our church. People with cancer were healed. Tumors disappeared. People with life-threatening illnesses got up and walked out of the hospital. We even had one doctor in our church who prayed over a patient already declared dead. Time of death had been called. But this physician knew the Great Physician, and he laid his hands on him, and in the name of Jesus that dead man came back to life! The whole medical community was in disbelief. (We ended up baptizing that man in the ocean after he gave his life to Jesus.)

So when the doctors gave us the report about our son, we went home and began listing all the mighty miracles we had seen God do in our midst, and we asked Him to do that for Jefferson. We prayed. Our family prayed. Our small group prayed, but we didn't just pray. We got Jefferson to the best therapists we could find. Julie radically adjusted her life and dedicated herself to getting our son the best help we could. *We worked as if it was all up to us, and we prayed as if it was all up to God.* We needed a miracle.

The Long Way Around

Sometimes God does a miracle in a minute, and sometimes He takes you on a journey of miracles. We tend to prefer the miracle-in-a-minute route. It's quick. We can see the results instantaneously, and we can move on with our life. But I've found that God often prefers the journey of little miracles along the way. We were on the journey plan. It's important when you're praying for a miracle that you know which plan God has you signed up for. If all you're thinking about is the big, instantaneous miracle, you'll miss the mini miracles along the way. If all you're looking for is for the problem to be solved, the issue to go away, you'll miss the other work God is wanting to do in your life. I almost missed it.

What I wanted was the microwave miracle. God, please heal my son, now. What He had in store was something much different.

Day by day we began to see God work. We prayed for finances, because thirty to forty hours of therapy a week is expensive, and we saw God provide in the most remarkable ways. We prayed for the right friends to surround our family during this time, and God moved two amazing families right next door to us with kids that became like brothers and sisters to Jefferson. Their families' love carried us through those early years.

At four years old Jefferson did not speak much at all. He had a word here or there, but they were random words. I remember praying for him to put five words together in a sentence. Just five words. That week Julie took Jefferson to the mall, and a new Disney Store had just opened. Jefferson loved Disney. He ran up to the window and looked at the characters and shouted at the top of his lungs, "Look, Mom, Snow White and the seven *whores!*" Julie didn't care that her five-year-old son had just shouted *that word* across the entire mall. He had just put eight words together in one sentence! It was a journey of miracles.

During the following months and years Jefferson began to thrive. Eight words became eighty words, and soon he was in the back of the car talking nonstop. On one of our pilgrimages to Disney World he sat in the back seat and talked the entire three hours, which is a reminder to be careful what you pray for, because you might actually get it. But every word that came from his mouth was an answer to prayer. It was a journey of miracles.

> **Sometimes God does a miracle in a minute, and sometimes He takes you on a journey of miracles.**

One of the things we've learned about being on the journey of miracles is that more people get in on the story. Because God didn't heal Jefferson instantaneously when he was two or three years old, more people joined us on the journey. More people prayed with us. Cried with us. Rejoiced with us at his proclamation in the mall. More people have seen God healing Jefferson through the years, and it has built their faith. In fact, his journey has helped other families on their journeys. Our journey of miracles has built their faith.

When the Journey Makes a Detour

But one day all of that changed. When Jefferson was thirteen, he started experiencing unexplainable neurological and psychological episodes that caused him to regress and lose his will to live. The doctors ran dozens of tests but could not tell us what was happening to our son. He stopped talking. He stopped laughing. He stopped *being*. We saw the life drain out of our son's eyes. Our once happy-go-lucky, life-of-the-party son was gone. He didn't want to get out of bed. He didn't want to eat. He didn't want...anything.

All this happened as Julie and I were stepping up to be the senior pastors of our church. The demands and expectations of leading a large, multisite congregation while all this was taking place was overwhelming. It was one of the darkest and most difficult times we ever faced. It didn't last for a few weeks or even a few months. This unexplainable, doubt-inducing trauma went on for a few years. And it was in this season that my faith began to slip. I began to question God and everything I believed about Him.

> Doubt can build faith.

I questioned the miracles I read about and preached about. I questioned God's character and nature that would allow this to happen to our son after all he'd been through. I questioned if my prayers even mattered. Doubt wasn't just knocking *at* my door, it had knocked it down and stormed into our home and taken our family hostage.

I remember standing up to preach on Sundays, telling people about God's faithfulness, the power of prayer, and that nothing is too hard for God while at the same time wrestling to believe any of it myself. How could I do this? How could I lead a church, pastor people, when I was questioning everything I believed? Thoughts of stepping aside entered my mind: "Maybe I can't be the pastor of our church. Maybe I shouldn't be." I had forgotten in the dark what God had shown me in the light. I had forgotten about the revelation of His great love. If I had remembered, it might have carried me through this season. It might have given me hope to know that His love wouldn't let me go. His love wouldn't leave our son in this situation. But doubt had darkened my view and was trying to take me out.

This season of unanswered prayers, endless delays, and inexplicable detours would teach me a lot about doubt— how to identify it and deal with it in a healthy way. One of the most surprising lessons I learned is that God can handle our questions, and He invites us to the shouting matches. These times of soul-deep questioning can actually build our intimacy with Him. I learned that doubt can build faith. It can help you process *what* you believe and *why* you believe it. Parts of my faith had never been tested before—things I believed *just because* I grew up believing them. God was getting ready to use doubt to strengthen my faith, but it wasn't going to be a comfortable journey.

WORK OUT THE DOUBT

1. What miracle are you asking God to do in your life or in your family?

2. Do you feel as though you are on the miracle-in-a-minute path or the journey of miracles, and why?

3. Are there any mile markers on the miracle journey you may have missed while looking for the "big miracle"? Take a minute to write down the ways God has shown up that could have been overlooked.

Chapter 7

WHEN IT COMES TO FAITH, IT'S EASY TO DOUBT

When the men came to Jesus, they said, "John the Baptist sent us to you to ask, 'Are you the one who is to come, or should we expect someone else?'"
—LUKE 7:20, NIV

D OES GOD REALLY exist?

Do miracles still happen?

Does God hear my prayers?

We've all wrestled with these questions. When it comes to faith, it's easy to doubt. Doubt is our natural response to the supernatural. We are limited by what our minds can conceive and comprehend. The fact that something is "supernatural" literally means it is outside the natural realm, so doubt is the natural response.

When I was walking through my season of doubt, I didn't just question God, I questioned myself. I felt embarrassed and ashamed for the feelings I had, and I couldn't tell many people in my life about it. After all, I was their pastor! I've spoken with other Christians who also felt guilty when they doubted God. They wished their faith was stronger and thought perhaps God would have answered their prayers if it was. But God doesn't only answer our prayers when our faith is firm. He's at work even when our faith is flimsy.

One of the reasons we feel guilty is that we believe doubt is the opposite of faith. Not true. Doubt happens *because* of faith. Without faith there would be no reason for doubt. Remember, doubt is defined as a feeling of uncertainty or questioning a belief you hold. And when it comes to faith, doubt is often described as a lack of confidence or trust in God. Doubt obviously suggests there is a lack of faith somewhere, but a person can doubt and still have faith in God. Doubt is a *place* of uncertainty, an *area* in your faith life that doesn't make sense. And the incongruence is causing a spiritual disruption.

But just because you doubt God in one area does not mean your faith in Him completely disappears. It means you're working to understand your faith at a deeper level. I believe that when dealt with properly, doubt can lead to faith. It can force us to wrestle with what we believe and why we believe it. It causes us to seek what is true and right.

DOUBTERS ANONYMOUS

I used to think that great men and women in the Bible never doubted God. But when I read the Scriptures, I find the exact opposite is true. Abraham doubted God's promise to bless him and make him the father of many nations. David questioned God when his prayers went unanswered. Even John the Baptist—who baptized Jesus in the Jordan River and saw the heavens open up and the Holy Spirit descend and heard the audible voice of God say, "This is my Son, whom I love; with him I am well pleased"

(Matt. 17:5, NIV)—doubted Jesus. And the disciples, who were eyewitnesses to hundreds of miracles, doubted that same Jesus when they saw Him crucified on the cross.

One of Jesus' disciples is known for his doubt; it's his claim to fame. Even if you haven't read much of the Bible, you've probably heard of Doubting Thomas. Thomas wasn't at the empty tomb on that first Easter morning. He wasn't there the first time Jesus revealed Himself in His resurrected body to the disciples. So when they gathered in an upper room the week after the resurrection, Thomas was filled with fear and doubts.

Thomas had been there when Jesus raised Lazarus from the dead. He had witnessed the feeding of the multitudes with a boy's small lunch. He had seen Jesus open blinded eyes and heal crippled legs. For three years he had a front-row seat to the miraculous—and still he doubted Jesus because the situation didn't play out the way he thought it would, or the way he thought it *should*.

Maybe you can relate to Thomas. Life isn't turning out the way you wanted it to or the way you had prayed or planned. And it feels as if God has let you down. That's exactly what Thomas was feeling. Think about it: He had given up everything to follow Jesus. He had left his career, his family, his home to follow this man he *thought* was the Messiah, the one he *thought* would overthrow the Roman Empire and establish His earthly kingdom and rule. Surely He wouldn't die on a cross between two thieves. It didn't turn out the way Thomas expected. Jesus had let him down.

Doubts often come when our expectations of God go unmet, when God doesn't come through the way we asked Him to or the way we expected He would. When we believe God is going to act a certain way, provide in a certain manner, or heal by a certain time and He doesn't come through *that way*, we're disappointed. And disappointment opens the door to doubt.

DISAPPOINTMENT'S DIVERSION

As I look back on my struggle with doubt, disappointment has always been a key player. In Jefferson's story I was disappointed that God had let this happen to him in the first place. Why couldn't God have protected him? I was disappointed that God hadn't already healed Jefferson. What was He waiting for? I was disappointed that Jefferson seemed to be getting worse every day, not better. God was letting me down.

If we're honest, we've all struggled with being disappointed by God. We do all the right things. Pray all the right prayers. And still God doesn't come through for us. It seems as though the prayer went unanswered, the need unmet, and as a result we blame God. But disappointment doesn't come from God. *God cannot disappoint. God can only appoint.* God has a purpose and plan for your life, an appointment for you. Disappointment is trying to move you in the opposite direction of your appointment.

The prefix *dis* negates whatever it precedes. *Dis*trust means that trust is broken. *Dis*unity is moving in the opposite direction of unity. And in the same way, *dis*appointment moves you in the opposite direction of your God-given appointment and assignment, trying to get you offtrack from your God-given destiny. In my season of doubt, my disappointment in God was trying to dislodge me from my relationship with Him and the purpose He had for my life.

Thomas allowed his disappointment to open the door to doubt. But we read in the Gospel of John that

> eight days later the disciples were together again, and this time Thomas was with them. The doors were locked; but suddenly, as before, Jesus was standing among them. "Peace be with you," he said. Then he said to Thomas, "Put your finger here, and look at my hands. Put your hand into the wound in my side. Don't be faithless any longer. Believe!" "My Lord and my God!" Thomas exclaimed.
>
> —JOHN 20:26–28

There are a few lessons we can learn from our friend Thomas whenever we're struggling with doubt:

1. When you don't know what to think, you can know where to go.

Thomas was dealing with doubt, but he wasn't hanging out with other doubters. He was with people who had seen something he had not seen, who had experienced something he had not experienced.

Think about it. Where was Thomas when his doubting began? He obviously wasn't with the other disciples. They all encountered Jesus after His resurrection, but Thomas wasn't there. We don't know where he was, but he wasn't with his brothers. He was separated from them, and his isolation kept him from the revelation that Jesus was alive. Our spiritual enemy plays the same game with us. He tries to keep you separated from the people who can help you build your faith.

Often when we are struggling with our faith, we pull away from people who are actually strong in their faith, either from embarrassment or intimidation. But that's illogical, right? It would be like staying away from the doctor's office when you're sick or avoiding the grocery store when you need food. When you're struggling with doubt, don't push away from people whose faith is strong. When doubt is taking you out, hang out with people of faith.

The apostle Paul writes in Romans 1:12 (NCV), "I want us to help each other with the faith we have. Your faith will help me, and my faith will help you." Paul is sharing a vital secret when it comes to dealing with doubt. He says there will be times when your faith is low and doubt is knocking at your door. When that happens, lean into the faith of a friend. Let their faith fuel your faith. Let their prayers carry you. Paul also says there will be times when others' faith will be low, and it will be your faith that carries them. So the next time you feel your faith growing weak, hang out with people whose faith is strong. Let their faith cause you to hold on to God and His promises. Let their faith help you believe.

> Disappointment is trying to move you in the opposite direction of your appointment.

When I was in my darkest days of doubt, I purposefully surrounded myself with people of faith. Julie and I stayed close to my parents and a few trusted friends in the church. The guys in my small group carried me spiritually. When I didn't want to pray or know what to pray, they prayed. They reminded me of what God did when Jefferson was four and five and ten years old. They had witnessed the journey of miracles and reminded me that if God had done it then, He could do it now.

DON'T WAIT FOR THE STORM

Julie and I live in South Florida, and every summer we have the threat of hurricanes. At the beginning of summer the news stations remind us we are entering hurricane season, and they warn their viewers to prepare ahead of time. They provide lists of critical supplies to have on hand so that when a storm is coming, you'll be prepared. If you wait until the storm is just a few days away, all the flashlights and batteries at the hardware store will be gone, and you'll be left in the dark.

So it is with faith-filled friends. You don't get those overnight from Amazon. You can't just run to the store and buy them when the storm is approaching. They take time to cultivate. Don't wait until you need the faith of a friend to get a friend who has faith. If the people around you don't know how to pray, you need to get some new friends. If the people around you don't know how to stand on the truth of God's Word and declare faith over your storm, you need to find friends who can.

In the meantime, God has created a place where you can lean on the faith of others—His family. The church is God's family, and family is a place where you can borrow things. When Jefferson turned fifteen, he hit a growth spurt. Instantly he and I were wearing the same size shoes and shirts. It wasn't unusual for me to show up at church and see him wearing my favorite sneakers or a shirt I had just bought. But it was OK because we're family. He could go into my room and borrow anything he wanted.

In the church there will be times when you need to "go into the room" and borrow someone else's faith. There are people who have walked with God longer than you have. They've seen things you haven't seen. Borrow their faith. Get around people who are wiser than you and borrow their godly wisdom. When you're feeling spiritually weak and can't go on, get around some people who are spiritually strong and borrow their strength. Don't miss out on the faith in God's family. Don't wait for the storm.

2. When you're dealing with doubt, reach out for Jesus.

The next lesson we learn from Thomas is what happens in John 20:27: "Then [Jesus] said to Thomas, 'Put your finger here, and look at my hands. Put your hand into the wound in my side. Don't be faithless any longer. Believe!'"

> Don't wait until you need the faith of a friend to get a friend who has faith.

Sometimes in our doubt we push God away. We get angry with Him and blame Him for something that has happened in our lives. Instead of reaching out for God, we reach out for anything to silence the doubt and numb the pain. Some reach for alcohol, or ice cream, or binge-watch a miniseries on TV to try to fill the spiritual emptiness inside. Some reach out to other doubters to try to justify their doubts, or they reach out to their online communities to vent instead of heal. But *Thomas reached out for Jesus*. His movement was toward Christ, and the Bible promises that when you move toward God, He moves toward you (James 4:8).

I remember days when I pushed God away. I was so disappointed He hadn't already healed Jefferson that I thought, "Fine, then I'm not going to talk to You anymore."

As if giving God the silent treatment was going to help me or the situation. It ended up making me feel more isolated and alone. After several days I turned back to God. I didn't have anywhere else to turn. I was desperate for Him to do something. Anything.

What I love about Jesus is that anytime you reach out for Him, He's reaching back for you. His arms are wide open. No judgment. No condemnation. No rejection. In this story, Jesus didn't reprimand Thomas. He didn't try to shame him in front of the other disciples. He just told Thomas to reach out and touch Him.

This encounter between Thomas and Jesus tells us it's OK to question God. He can handle it. It's OK to struggle with spiritual doubt; we all do. In fact, doubt might actually be good for you because it means you are seeking truth. A lesson I learned years ago has helped me in my seasons of doubt:

- Take your doubts and turn them into questions.

- Take your questions and turn them into prayers.

- Take your prayers and let them turn you to God.

If your doubts cause you to seek truth, that journey will always lead you closer to God, because God is truth. God promises in Jeremiah 29:13, "You will seek me and find me when you seek me with all your heart." That's an amazing promise I've had to hold on to, because the journey to find God and figure out what He's doing takes longer than you think.

WORK OUT THE DOUBT

1. Do you relate to Thomas when he allowed disappointment to open the door for doubt? Finish the thought:

   I was disappointed when God...

2. Who are the people who fuel faith in your life?

3. What is one thing Thomas did right when he was processing his doubts, and how can you do the same?

Chapter 8

DELAY: DOUBT'S ACCOMPLICE

Delays are as much a part of God's plan as answered prayers.
—RICK WARREN

THOSE DARK MONTHS when Jefferson had become a shell of his former self seemed to go on forever. We were constantly sitting in doctor's offices waiting for someone to tell us what was wrong and how we could fix our son. We spent countless hours in waiting rooms. Waiting for test results. Waiting for bloodwork. Waiting for answers. Waiting for anything that would give us a glimmer of hope that God was hearing our prayers.

I've grown to hate waiting rooms. Spaces created for the sole purpose of waiting. I'm not very good at waiting. It's never been my strong suit. When I pull up to a red light, I evaluate the cars in front of me to determine which one looks faster so I can get behind it. When I'm at the grocery store, I examine my options: which carts have fewer items and which cashier looks most enthusiastic about their job. Anything to reduce the wait.

The problem is we often see waiting as wasted time. Surely there is something better we could be doing than just sitting here waiting. Research indicates I'm not alone. Because of the rapid advancement of technology and the constant availability of instant gratification, our modern society struggles with waiting. Our attention spans decreased from twelve seconds in the year 2000 to just eight seconds in 2013, shorter than that of a goldfish.[1] And they remain at that level today. As a result, any delay negatively impacts our mental and emotional well-being, leading to increased anxiety and stress.[2]

Yet sometimes God does His greatest work in the waiting room of life, that space when it feels like your life is on hold. It's there that God gets our attention. Isaiah 40:31 (NKJV) promises, "But those who wait on the LORD shall renew their strength; they shall mount up with wings like eagles, they shall run and not be weary, they shall walk and not faint." Waiting isn't just about what we hope to receive but about who we will become.

DAVID THE DOUBTER

There's a guy in the Bible who spent a lot of time waiting, and his delays led to doubt. David not only had his doubts about God, he wrote them down for us to read. Many of the psalms are a record of David's disbelief and questions about God. Often when we think about David, we remember his battle with Goliath. A small shepherd boy takes down a mighty giant with just a slingshot and a small stone. A picture of a conqueror. A champion. A superhero. But that's not the beginning of David's story.

To understand David you must rewind the superhero movie a bit. In 1 Samuel 16 we read of the prophet Samuel hearing from God and going to anoint the next king over Israel. The Spirit of God leads him to Bethlehem, a small farming town just six miles south of Jerusalem. It's interesting that Bethlehem would be the place where the future king of Israel would come from. The same fields where the angels would announce the birth of the Messiah to a group of shepherds hundreds of years later. The same place where Mary would give birth to the Son of God. This same town is the place where the prophet goes to anoint the king of Israel, a foreshadowing of our coming King.

When the prophet arrives at the house of Jesse, David's father, he asks Jesse to bring his sons out so he can pray over them. Jesse lines up his seven sons in front of the prophet. Samuel prays over them, but none of them are to be the next king. So Samuel asks Jesse, "Do you have any more sons?" and Jesses remembers he has one more. "What's his name, Danny? Don? No... David." So they run to get David, who was taking care of the sheep in a field, forgotten by his own father.

David runs in from the field and stands before the prophet. God speaks to Samuel and confirms that David is to be the next king of Israel. Samuel takes the oil and anoints David, blesses him, and prays over him in front of his whole family. Can you imagine how significant that experience must have been to him? The prophet of the nation comes to your house and anoints you as the future king. It had to be unreal. David had to be thinking, "Now everything is going to change. No more sheep duty for me. Maybe I'll get a little respect around here and my dad will remember my name." But when you read the story of David's life, this encounter put him on a journey of waiting. Scholars believe David was a teenager when he was anointed to be king. But he doesn't *become* king for another twenty-five years!

Twenty-five years of detours and delays. In fact, right after this remarkable moment David is sent back into the same field to look after the sheep. He would spend years in those fields before confronting Goliath. After killing the giant, David becomes a national hero. He had to be thinking, "OK, now…now's the time. Now I will get what I've been promised." No. He ends up in the court of King Saul as a servant, playing music for the king. Basically, David is the hired help, and the king is a little crazy. Saul becomes jealous of David and starts throwing his spears at him. David becomes King Saul's personal dartboard. I can imagine David sitting in the palace, having spears thrown at him, playing his harp, and thinking, "This is not how I thought it was going to turn out!"

Have you ever felt that way? Have you ever thought, "This is not how I thought my life was going to turn out? This is not how I thought my family would turn out… how that relationship would end. I didn't see this coming." We've all been there. Maybe you're there right now. Maybe you're in the middle of a marriage that has fallen apart. A business that has failed. A financial or health issue that has gone from bad to worse. This was David's story. He had to be wondering if the prophet got it wrong. Nothing was going the way he thought it would.

When Delay Turns to Doubt

Just when he thinks it can't get any worse, David is kicked out of the palace and goes on the run from Saul, who is trying to kill him. For years he's hiding in caves. Years of delay. Years on the run. Years of thinking, "When will I experience everything I have been promised?"

Many of us have the same questions. We are holding on to a promise of God, a scripture in the Bible that we believe (or once believed) was God's word for our lives. We've been praying for that broken relationship, for our child to be healed, for our career to take off, and it seems that God is not coming through on His promise. I understand. I've been there more times than I can count. I've been praying some prayers for more than two decades, and I still haven't seen them completely answered. Let me remind you of a lesson I've had to learn in my seasons of waiting: *God's delays are not God's denials.* Let that sink in. God's delays are not God's denials. Just because God is saying "not now" doesn't mean He has said no.

Don't get me wrong. Sometimes God *does* say no. He knows things we do not know. He sees things we cannot see. And sometimes no is exactly the answer we need. But "not now" doesn't mean no. Sometimes God has us in a waiting room for a long time.

And if God has you waiting, you're in good company. Joseph had to wait thirteen years before he realized the dreams God had put in his heart. Abraham had to wait twenty-five years for the promise of Isaac to be born. And Abraham didn't receive that promise until he was seventy-five years old. Seventy-five! You would think God could pick up His pace a bit, right? Moses had to wait forty years on the backside of a mountain until God said, "OK, I'm ready to use you now. Go set my people free." Even Jesus had to wait thirty years before He started His public ministry. If you're in God's waiting room, look around; you're in good company.

Most people I know that have been used by God in big ways have spent a lot of time in waiting rooms. If you feel as if something is seriously delayed, God may be getting ready to do something really big in your life. Don't give up during the delay. God's timing is perfect. He's never late, but He's rarely early. He's never dropped the ball on anyone, and He's not going to start with you.

This is difficult to remember during the delay. It's in the delay that we start to doubt. "Is God still there? Does He hear my prayers? Does He even care?" Delay sets the stage for doubt. Delay is doubt's accomplice, the co-conspirator that usually shows up right before doubt arrives. It prepares the platform for questioning God. We know this because David wrote many of the psalms expressing his doubts because of the delay. "O LORD, how long will you forget me? Forever? How long will you look the other way? How long must I struggle with anguish in my soul, with sorrow in my heart every day? How long will my enemy have the upper hand?" (Ps. 13:1–2).

> If you're in God's waiting room, look around; you're in good company.

When you're in life's waiting room, *doubt* is hanging out. Doubt will come and whisper in your ear, "I wonder why God isn't answering your prayers? I wonder why this is happening to you?" It's in the wait that we begin to wonder. It's in the delay that we begin to doubt. "God, why haven't I gotten married yet? Why can't we get pregnant? Why haven't You healed my friend?" Delay sets the stage for doubt. And if you're not careful this kind of doubt will cause you to walk away from God. Maybe not reject Him completely, but walk away from praying consistently because you're not getting the answers you want. Or you take the controls out of His hands and try to make things happen with or without God.

One of the saddest things I experience as a pastor is watching people give up on their faith. They get weary in the waiting when God doesn't come through *when* they want or the *way* they want, and the enemy uses doubt to sabotage their faith. They find themselves in a pit of despair—without the lifeline of faith-filled brothers and sisters around them to lift them up—and their faith dies in the delay.

WHAT YOU DO IN THE DELAY MATTERS

Even though David wasn't perfect and made lots of mistakes, he didn't let doubt or delay take him out. Even though Psalm 13 starts out with words of doubt, it doesn't end there. He goes on to say, "But I trust in your unfailing love. I will rejoice because you have rescued me. I will sing to the LORD because he is good to me" (Ps. 13:5–6). Notice David says "I *will* rejoice" and "I *will* sing." It was a decision he made. He learned a lesson we need to learn: Don't allow your feelings to derail your faith. David doesn't go by what he feels. He goes by what he knows. And more specifically by *who* he knows. And that decision leads to worship. David worshipped in the wait. Right there in the middle of that waiting room he began to worship. "I will sing of your goodness. I will declare your faithfulness." What you do during your delay matters.

SMALL BEGINNINGS

You may have heard some of the story of Christ Fellowship Church. My parents started our church in their living room with twenty people back in the 1980s. Soon we outgrew our living room and moved to a small elementary school "cafetorium"—part cafeteria, part auditorium. We would spend the next seven years setting up and tearing down in that small school, growing the church to seventy people. Only seventy people after seven years. Kids and all. That was counting pregnant women twice.

I can promise you we dealt with doubt during those years of delay. "God, why are we stuck in this school with only seventy people? For seven years? We've got more in us that this! The dream and vision you put in our heart is bigger than this." It would have been easy to let doubt take us out, to shut the door

> **Delay sets the stage for doubt.**

on the dream and vision of starting this church, but my parents did not let the delay derail their faith. Every week my dad preached and pastored those seventy people as if they were seven hundred.

After seven years of delay, God began to open doors. We found an old horse farm and converted a barn into a worship center. Within a few years we had over four thousand people crammed into that barn every weekend. Then we bought a cow field across the street to build a bigger facility. Within a few years that four thousand doubled to eight thousand people every weekend, and the bigger building wasn't big enough to contain what God was wanting to do. His dream for us was actually bigger than ours.

Looking back, we realized the delay was for our development. God was preparing us to be used in ways we never could have imagined. When my parents first planted the church, we couldn't have handled that kind of growth. We wouldn't have been ready for it. So God was getting us ready. He was working on our character. He was removing any inclination of self-reliance and independence. He was keeping us on our knees, humbled and desperate for Him to move and provide. God wanted to make sure that when Christ Fellowship took off, we knew *who* was making it happen, and it wasn't us. God used the delay for our good.

BATTING CAGE OR BENCH?

I have discovered in my times of waiting that it often feels like I'm being sidelined. It seems as if everyone else is moving forward and I'm in the dugout, sitting on the bench. In moments like that, we each have a choice to make. Are we going to sit on the bench or get in the batting cage and get ready for what God is getting us ready for?

Getting in the batting cage is making the most of the wait. It's a step of faith that says, "God, I don't know when You'll put me in the game, but I will be ready when You call my name." Getting in the batting cage says I'm going to get better during a season of waiting. Waiting won't slow me down or take me out. It will be an opportunity to get prepared for the promises that are coming my way.

During times in my life and ministry when I felt like I was being sidelined, I had a decision to make. How can I leverage this delay for my development? How can I use this time to become better, stronger? My transition into senior leadership was delayed a few times. Situations out of my control pushed the pause button on me becoming the senior pastor of our church. I remember one time when that delay led to discouragement. My dad picked up on it and coached me to get ready for what God was getting ready to do in my life. He challenged me to get in the batting cage and go back to seminary. I had completed my master's but hadn't considered going after my doctorate. I took his advice and went back to school. I was able to earn my doctorate in theology, but more importantly I was growing as a student of the Word. The classes challenged my thinking and understanding of Scripture. The process of finishing my education, while having a full-time job and being a husband and faither, stretched me as a person. It required a new level of self-discipline and focus, all by-products of the delay. God used the delay for my development.

Waiting is inevitable. Delays will be a part of the journey. In fact, sometimes the delay is as important as the destination because of what God wants to do in the wait. Your dream from God may not be to start a church or become a pastor. The promise you're holding onto probably isn't just like mine, but you have one. Hold on to it. Don't let delay derail your faith. Get in the batting cage and start warming up.

WORK OUT THE DOUBT

1. What areas of your life feel delayed?

2. What promises of God are you holding on to?

3. Do you feel like you are on the bench or in the batting cage? How can you get in the batting cage and actively pursue growth and prepare for God's next assignment?

Chapter 9

DETOURS: WHY BAD THINGS HAPPEN TO GOOD PEOPLE

*The path you'd never choose can lead to
the faith you've always wanted.*
—Lori Ann Wood

N OBODY LIKES DETOURS, the large orange signs telling you that you cannot go where you need to go. Detours disrupt our planned course of action and force us down roads we never intended to travel. They delay the journey and add frustration and uncertainty to the itinerary.

When Christ Fellowship was small and Julie and I were the youth pastors, we would load our students in a fifteen-passenger van and head to summer youth camp in Indiana. Along the way we would do some whitewater rafting and hit a few theme parks. One night as we were driving through the mountains of North Carolina, we came upon a detour forcing us off the main road. We were trying to get to our hotel in Boone before it got dark so we could eat dinner, get everyone settled in their rooms, and be ready for a great day of rafting the next morning. The detour took us off a state highway (which was nothing more than a glorified, two-lane road) and put us on a road that seemed like it hadn't been paved since 1956. It was dark, and several times Julie and I were convinced we were lost in the middle of the Appalachian Mountains with a group of starving teenagers.

The students started asking questions. They were certain I had gotten us all lost. They were hungry and needed to use the restroom. It's funny how you need to *go* when there is no place to *go*. There were no gas stations. No places to stop and ask for directions so I could assure everyone (and myself) that we were on the right road. Just farms and hills. After about an hour on that country road, we made our way back to the highway and stopped at the first restroom we could find. Crisis averted. The detour was frustrating and a bit inconvenient, but it was forgotten by the next day.

DETOURS IN LIFE TEND TO LAST LONGER

It's one thing when you get stuck on a detour in the back hills of North Carolina. It's another thing when you find yourself on a detour in life, headed down a road you didn't choose, feeling a bit disoriented and frustrated. Those kinds of detours tend to last more than a couple of hours. Often, life's detours can lead us to a totally different destination.

Our family's life was forever changed by that one doctor's report concerning Jefferson's diagnosis. It sent us on a road we had not planned to travel. A road we would never choose. In many ways the detour forged a new destination for our lives.

Maybe you're on a detour that is taking your life in a direction you didn't plan. A divorce you didn't see coming. An illness that has defined your life and your family. A business venture that failed. It's more than a delay that will soon be over; it's a detour off the predetermined path you had for your life, and it seems like it's taking you in a totally different direction than you wanted to go.

A Fair Question

If you're like me, detours cause you to question God. As I traveled this road with Jefferson, the one question I found myself repeatedly asking was: If God is so good and so powerful, why is He letting this happen to us, and why can't He make it go away? As a pastor, it's one of the most common questions I'm asked by people who are facing some of life's darkest moments. If God is so good, why do bad things happen? It's an honest question. A fair question. A question God can handle.

Anytime we question God we have to start with Scripture. The Bible is God's revelation of Himself to humanity. The answer to every question you have about God is found in its pages. There are four truths we see from the account of creation in Genesis that help us begin to grapple with this question.

First, when God created the world, *it was good.* In the beginning, when God created the heavens and the earth, the rivers and the fields, He said, "It is good." When God created the planet we live on, there were no earthquakes, no tornadoes, no floods, no crime or sickness or death. It was paradise.

Second, *God gave man the ability to choose.* God created mankind in His image and set us apart from all of creation. He gave us a God-consciousness and the ability to make moral choices.

Third, *people chose evil.* Adam and Eve chose to disobey God. Go their own way. God said one thing, they did the opposite. And ultimately that choice had lasting consequences. Romans 5:12 tells us that when Adam sinned, sin and death entered the world. Later in Romans 8, it says that creation was "subjected to frustration [by sin]" and is groaning for the return of Christ. Since the fall of man, when sin entered the world, all of creation has been longing, groaning, waiting for the return of Christ, when pain and suffering will cease.

One other foundational truth as we approach this question is that Jesus never promised we wouldn't have problems or struggles. In fact, He promised that we would. He said, "In this world you will have trouble, but take heart, I have overcome the world"

> **If God is so good, why do bad things happen?**

(John 16:33). Jesus didn't say we *might* have troubles, but that we *will* have trouble. The word *trouble* in the original language means oppression, affliction, tribulation, persecution. This isn't trouble like the Wi-Fi is down, or I have a flat tire. This is serious suffering. Jesus said it's guaranteed. But He also says don't be overwhelmed by it, because He has overcome the world.

All throughout the Bible we witness bad things happening to good people. Joseph was sold into slavery by his brothers. Daniel was thrown into the lions' den for praying. David had spears thrown at him for killing a giant and saving a nation. But the poster child for bad things happening to good people is a guy named Job. If you're ever feeling bad about your life, just read about Job. It will encourage you.

Job was a good man. A righteous man. The Bible says he was blameless in the sight of God. We read that he was a wealthy man with a large family. Then one day everything changed. A fire fell from the sky and burned up his flocks. His enemies raided his barns. A tornado swept through his property and killed all his children. All in one day. Job was left with nothing.

When Job heard this news, the Bible says,

> Job stood up and tore his robe in grief. Then he shaved his head and fell to the ground to worship. He said, "I came naked from my mother's womb, and I will be naked when I leave. The LORD gave me what I had, and the LORD has taken it away. Praise the name of the LORD!" In all of this, Job did not sin by blaming God.
>
> —Job 1:20–22

That was just the first chapter! Throughout the Book of Job things go from bad to worse. His friends turn against him. His own wife tells him to "curse God and die" (she's a real encouragement). Job's life took a turn he never saw coming. This was more than a minor inconvenience; this was a series of life-altering events that would steer Job down a whole new path. But in the end the detour brought him closer to God. At the very end of the book, Job says to God, "My ears had heard of you, but now my eyes have seen you" (42:5, NIV). Read that verse again: "My ears had heard of you but now my eyes have seen you." Before this trial Job had *heard* of God. He had heard of His power and presence, but after this trial he had a firsthand encounter with God. He *saw* God.

There are a few lessons I have learned on my detour:

Your Pain Can Push You Closer to God

We said in the last chapter that tribulation can lead to revelation. Pain can push you closer to God. But it can also push you away from God if you let it. The choice is yours. Instead of lying on the ground crying in bitterness, Job cried out to God. When you read the Book of Job, you see that he was full of emotions. At times he was angry with God, yelling at Him. Other times he yelled *to* God. But he didn't allow his pain to push him away from God. Pain will either come between you and God or bind you to God. It's your choice.

The verse that has always stood out to me from Job's story is found at the end of chapter 1: "In all of this, Job did not sin by blaming God" (v. 22). Job did not blame God for the pain he faced. So often we do blame God. In our pain, we're prone to point our finger at God. Shake our fist toward heaven. Somehow accuse God for the trial we're going through. We indict Him for not caring, for not being there for us. But I've learned that *the presence of a problem does not mean the absence of my God.* Just because I'm facing a problem doesn't mean God is gone. I have found He is even closer in our pain. Psalm 34:18 (NIV) reminds us, "The LORD is close to the brokenhearted and saves those who are crushed in spirit." God doesn't promise to protect us from our problems. He promises His presence in the middle of our problems. He will be with you no matter what you're facing.

Julie and I have faced many tough challenges through the years. At times I've questioned why God was allowing this trial to happen to us. At first I allowed my doubts and pain to push me away from God, but that only left me feeling more hopeless and afraid. I needed God. I needed His strength and wisdom if I was going to make it on this detour. Psalm 46:1 (NIV) says, "God is our refuge and strength, an ever-present help in trouble." When you're in trouble, God is "ever-present"—always there. Let your pain push you closer to Him.

YOUR PAIN CAN HELP OTHERS FIND GOD

Not only can your pain push you closer to God, but it can help others find God. When you walk through a storm with a supernatural peace, holding on to your faith in Christ no matter what, that shouts of God's power and grace in your life. It's easy to be full of faith when everything is going your way.

> Tribulation can lead to revelation.

Everyone's healthy. Bills are all paid. Business is good. But when things are falling apart and you're still full of faith, that points to something supernatural. It grabs people's attention.

Have you ever witnessed someone walk through a trial full of faith in God? You look at what they're facing and wonder, "How are they doing that? It seems other-worldly." Because it is! We have a family in our church who have walked through countless struggles and persecutions. Juan and Alicia Szuka have faced more hardships than any family I know, yet their faith in God is solid. Juan and Alicia have two amazing daughters, Cynthia and Elisabeth, both with special needs. Cynthia was born at twenty-nine weeks, weighing less than three pounds. Her doctors said she wouldn't live more than one day. But one day turned into two, which turned into five weeks when the doctors sent her home. As a baby, Cynthia developed many physical complications and was diagnosed with cerebral palsy. Again, doctors warned her parents that Cynthia would not live a long life and would spend most of it bedridden. But Cynthia defied the doctors' reports. She graduated from high school and went on to graduate from college at the top of her class. She writes Bible curriculum for other children with special needs. Cynthia is now thirty-eight years old!

Her sister, Elisabeth, has a visual and central auditory processing disorder and faces her own set of challenges. And their father, Juan, was diagnosed with hydrocephalus and recently lost his ability to walk on his own. Any family facing so many challenges could have every right to gripe and complain. "God why me? Why haven't you heard our prayers and healed our daughters? Why is all this happening to our family?" But instead of getting consumed with the *why* the Szukas focused on the *what*. "God, what do You want to do with this pain? How are You going to use it? What is Your plan for us now?"

Instead of focusing on their pain, they focused on their purpose, and out of their suffering God has birthed ministries for other families with special needs. The Szuka family started a Special Needs Ministry at our church that has served thousands of children and families with disabilities. Partnering with Wheels for the World, Cynthia spearheaded the collection of used wheelchairs and walkers for people in need. To date she has collected and sent *more than twenty-three thousand wheelchairs and*

walkers to people in underdeveloped nations of the world—
each one sent with a Bible attached!

Their faith has shouted of God's faithfulness. Their
pain has pushed people closer to God, helping them find
God. Their pain had a divine purpose, and their detour
took them to a new destination, a destination where thousands of people were waiting on them.

YOUR PAIN WILL MAKE YOU MORE LIKE JESUS

God uses the detours and delays in our life to refine us.
Romans 8:28 is a familiar scripture often quoted to help
give courage in times of uncertainty. "And we know that
God causes everything to work together for the good of
those who love God and are called according to his purpose for them."

This verse is filled with certainty. It says we *know*, not
we hope. Not we think or wish, but we can be certain
that "God causes all things to work together." Even when
we can't see it, He's working. He is the Master Designer,
working everything—even the mistakes, the hurts, the
disappointments—all together for our good. It doesn't
say that everything will *be* good or *feel* good. It may be
painful, but God will work it *for* our good.

Remember, these words were not written by someone
who was insulated from pain and suffering. This was Paul,
who had been beaten and shipwrecked, left for dead and
imprisoned. He knew trouble. And He tells us that God
will work it all together for our good.

Most people stop reading that passage at the end of verse
28 with a simple hope that somehow all the bad things
in their life will turn out good. But to fully understand

the text, you have to read it in context. The big idea of this passage continues in the next verse. Paul first says that God causes all things to work together for the good of those who love God. But he continues, "For God knew His people in advance and He chose them to *become like his Son*" (Rom. 8:29, NIV, emphasis added). What is the good God is working toward? To make us more like Jesus. To shape us into the image and character of Christ.

You may have heard the story of when Michelangelo unveiled his famous sculpture of David. A man asked, "How…could you have achieved a masterpiece like this from a crude slab of marble?" Michelangelo responded, "It was easy. All I did was chip away everything that didn't look like David."[1] That's what God does to us. He is the Master Artist in our lives, and He wants to remove everything that doesn't look like Jesus. The chipping away process can be painful.

I've experienced this in my life. God uses the difficulties and detours to expose areas in my life He wants to change. When I'm dealing with a problem I can't solve on my own, God brings me to a place of dependence on Him, chipping away at my self-sufficiency. When I am on a detour that makes me feel isolated or alone, God challenges me to look for others who might be in a similar place, calling me out of my self-absorption into a place of greater compassion for others. When I deal with rejection, it reminds me to look for others who feel rejected so I can be a source of encouragement to them.

In 2 Corinthians 1: 4–5, Paul reminds us that God is the source of our comfort.

> He comforts us in all our troubles so that we can
> comfort others. When they are troubled, we will be
> able to give them the same comfort God has given
> us. For the more we suffer for Christ, the more God
> will shower us with his comfort through Christ.

God wants His nature and grace to move through our lives toward others. What we've received from Him, He wants us to give away. The more suffering we go through, the more comfort and grace we have to give to others. God cares more about your character than your comfort, so He will allow uncomfortable things to come into your life to shape your character. When He does, don't waste the pain; let it make you more like Jesus.

ARE WE THERE YET?

When it comes to the question "Why do bad things happen to good people?" this final answer is extremely important to understand. We aren't *there* yet. This earth is not our home. This isn't heaven. So often we make the mistake and treat this place like it's our home. It's not. The Bible is clear that we are pilgrims passing through.

Sometimes when we face troubles and hardships, we look for deep theological reasons for the suffering when we need to simply remember that we live on a planet that is no longer good as God made it. The world is fallen, and the powers of evil are at work. Every time we deal with suffering, it needs to remind us we aren't home yet.

> Therefore, we do not lose heart. Though outwardly
> we are wasting away, yet inwardly we are being
> renewed day by day. For our light and momentary

troubles are achieving for us an eternal glory that
far outweighs them all. So we fix our eyes not on
what is seen, but on what is unseen, since what is
seen is temporary, but what is unseen is eternal.
—2 CORINTHIANS 4:16–18, NIV

Years ago Julie and I were visiting a woman in the hospital who was fighting cancer. Gail was a wife, mother, and grandmother, and she had been battling this disease for years. The doctors weren't giving her much hope. As we prayed with her that day, she told us with a smile on her face, "I'm in a win-win situation. If I'm healed, I win. I'll have more time with my family. And if I die, I win, because I get to go see Jesus." Gail got it. She understood that heaven was her home. Heaven is God's final answer to pain and suffering.

So those may be valid reasons for why bad things happen to good people, but what do I do when bad things happen to me? I have three challenges for you.

HOLD ON TO GOD

Jesus said, "Come to Me, all who are weary and heavy-laden, and I will give you rest" (Matt. 11:28, LSB). So many times when trouble hits we run to our friends, our therapist, our refrigerator. But Jesus says run to Me. Let the pain push you to Jesus.

"Is any one of you suffering? He should pray" (Jas. 5:13, BSB). When you pray, you are turning to the only One who can really do anything about the problem. When you pray, you're strengthening your connection with Jesus. When you pray, you're running to your strong tower and defense, your rock and fortress, so you will not be shaken. Even when everything around you is shaking, you will not be shaken.

HOLD ON TO GOD'S PROMISES

"Let us continue to hold firmly to the hope that we confess without wavering, for the one who made the promise is faithful" (Heb. 10:23, ISV). God promises He will never leave us or forsake us. He promises to never give us more than we can handle. He promises to walk with us through the darkest valleys. To give us strength when we're weary.

Hold on to those promises. Quote them back to God. "Lord, Your Word says You make a way where there seems to be no way, and I need You to make a way for me. Your Word promises that You will part the sea so I can walk right through it; that You have not given me a spirit of fear, so I stand in confidence and faith."

There are promises in God's Word I go back to constantly. There are promises I'm holding on to and quote back to God, not because God has forgotten them, but because I have the tendency to forget them. When I speak them out loud, it reminds my heart and mind of what is true. (I've listed some of the promises I use for different needs in my life in Appendix D.)

HOLD ON TO GOD'S PEOPLE

This is worthy of repeating because we tend to withdraw from the place God created to give us strength. When we go through struggle and suffering—even questioning God—we often pull back from people, either from a place of not wanting to share our problems or because we think we're the only one facing that kind of trouble. We find ourselves on a detour and feel isolated and alone. We said earlier that when you're struggling with doubt, hang out with people of faith. When you're on a detour of life, pick up the right traveling companions. Don't do the detour alone.

Sometimes the road you would never choose can build the faith you've always wanted. For our family, our detour has caused our faith and trust in God to grow. It has kept us desperate for His daily guidance and strength. I would never have chosen this detour for our family,

> **When you're on a detour of life, pick up the right traveling companions.**

but it has led us to a deeper place of encountering God. Like Job, I can say, "my ears have heard of You, but now I have seen You."

WORK OUT THE DOUBT

1. What detours in your life have you blamed on God?

_____ pushed me closer to
   God, because...

_____ pushed me away from
   God, because...

2. When has your pain pushed you *closer* to God, and when did it push you *away* from Him, and why?

3. What is one way you can prepare spiritually for the detours you don't see coming?

Chapter 10

DISTANCE: WHEN GOD IS SILENT

The instructor is always silent when the test is given.
—RICK WARREN

HAVE YOU EVER had a shouting match with God? I have. During the months when doctors told us there was nothing they could do for Jefferson, I found myself spending many days on my back porch, looking up to the sky and shouting my prayers. I was literally yelling my prayers at the top of my lungs. (I have no idea what my neighbors must have thought.)

The fear and anxiety I faced as a father was staggering. I was supposed to be the one to protect Jefferson, to solve the problems. Yet the physical and neurological troubles he was having paralyzed our family and forced me to pray like I've never prayed before.

It's amazing how you pray when you're desperate. There's no time for polite, neat prayers. No place for platitudes. Just a desperate cry for help. For me it was a shout. And as loud as I was, God seemed silent.

No response.

Not a word.

This continued for months. When I needed Him the most, God was quiet. All I wanted to hear was that my son would be OK, that Jefferson would come through this, that *we* would get through this. But all I received was silence.

As I shared earlier, this season rocked my faith. I was preaching on Sundays, questioning God Monday through Saturday. Standing up and telling people why they needed to trust God when I was having trouble trusting Him myself. At times it felt hypocritical.

I'm a pastor. I teach the Word of God to people, helping them know God in a deeper way so they can follow Him. I preach that God is a "speaking God." From the very beginning in Genesis, when God created the heavens and the earth, He spoke and said, "Let there be," and there was. All through the Bible we see God speaking to His people. Guiding them. Helping them know what to do.

John chapter 1 says, "In the beginning was the Word, and the Word was with God, and the Word was God.... The Word became flesh and made his dwelling among us. We have seen his glory, the glory of the one and only Son, who came from the Father, full of grace and truth" (vv. 1, 14). The very description of Jesus is "the Word"— God trying to communicate with us, speak to us. On the day of Pentecost in the Upper Room, when God poured out His Holy Spirit, the disciples spoke in a heavenly language. God communicating. Speaking through His Spirit.

THE SOUND OF SILENCE

If God is a speaking God, why are there times He seems so silent? Why does it seem as if the heavens are closed up? That my prayers go unanswered? God feels distant.

Many times in my walk with God I've experienced deafening silence. No whisper of the Holy Spirit. No confirmation of His presence. No answer to my prayers. And it's in the moments of silence where doubt shouts the loudest.

I remember when I got to the point where I didn't want to pray anymore. It didn't seem to be making a difference. Doubt was taking me out, pushing me further and further away from what I had believed my whole life. Countless times I had told people that God would always be there for them, never leave them or forsake them, but in those moments I felt forsaken. Alone.

But then I would look around and realize I wasn't alone. I had Julie's faith to lean on. Our friends and family surrounded us with their faith. The guys in my group from church, they hadn't gone anywhere. Remember Romans 1:12 (NCV), "I want

> **If God is a speaking God, why are there times He seems so silent?**

us to help each other with the faith we have. Your faith will help me, and my faith will help you." That's exactly what happened. When my doubt was louder than my faith, the faith of my friends showed up. When I couldn't pray anymore, they prayed for me. They stood in the gap and helped me build my faith back. They reminded me of what I knew, encouraged me to keep looking to God.

Earlier we looked at the prophet Elijah in 1 Kings 19. Right after he defeated the prophets of Baal on Mount Carmel, Queen Jezebel issued a threat and he went on the run. Hiding in a cave. Discouraged. Defeated. He even complained to God for the way he was being treated. He told God he was the only one left in the whole land of Israel trying to serve God. And God said to him,

> "Go out and stand on the mountain in the presence
> of the LORD, for the LORD is about to pass by." Then
> a great and powerful wind tore the mountains apart
> and shattered the rocks before the LORD, but the
> LORD was not in the wind. After the wind there was
> an earthquake, but the LORD was not in the earth-
> quake. After the earthquake came a fire, but the
> LORD was not in the fire. And after the fire came a
> gentle whisper. When Elijah heard it, he pulled his
> cloak over his face and went out and stood at the
> mouth of the cave.
>
> —1 KINGS 19:11–13, NIV

God spoke in a whisper. God loves to whisper. It's His
favorite form of communication. Yes, God used pillars of
cloud and fire to lead the Israelites through the wilderness. He parted the Red Sea to communicate His faithfulness to bring them out of Egypt and make a way. But His
favorite form of communication is a whisper. Think about
it. We whisper to people we are close to, people we have
a relationship with. It would be awkward and completely
inappropriate to go up to someone in the grocery store
and start whispering in their ear. A whisper isn't just for
people you're close with; a whisper requires that you get
close. That you turn down the noise around you to be able
to hear what's being said.

TO HEAR THE WHISPER, GET CLOSE TO THE WHISPERER

A whisper can only be heard in His presence, and there
are some things God wants to do in His presence that He
won't do any other place. There are some troubles that can
only be solved in His presence. There are some answers

we only find in His presence. In fact, everything we truly long for is found in His presence. That's the power of the whisper. It moves you into the presence of God.

My wife, Julie, is completely deaf in her left ear. She is officially hearing impaired, and she's been this way since she was a young child. This impairment has forced her to work her whole life to get in a position where she can hear the conversation. In

> **God loves to whisper. It's His favorite form of communication.**

meetings at church, she makes sure she gets a seat that will optimize her ability to hear what is said. If we go to a restaurant with a group of friends, Julie is diving for the seat at the end of the table so she can hear the conversation. If the restaurant is noisy, forget about it. The chances of her hearing what is being said decreases dramatically. Julie is constantly aware of her hearing impairment and continually working to put herself in a position to hear what people are saying.

I think most of us don't realize that we are spiritually hearing impaired. We wonder why we don't hear God speak more often or more clearly. Could it be that we aren't fighting to get into the position to hear Him? We aren't turning down the noise of life to hear His quiet whisper? To hear the whisper, you have to get close to the Whisperer.

A WHISPER IN THE WILDERNESS

When God wanted to speak to Abraham in Genesis 12, God had him leave his family and his home and led him into the wilderness. Abraham was living in a big city, with many people and distractions. God said, "Abraham, I want to speak to you. But in order for you to hear Me, you need to leave some things behind." And God begins to take Abraham and Sarah, and his nephew, Lot and his family with all their servants, through the wilderness toward the land of Canaan. The journey would have been long and arduous—sandy desert as far as the eye could see.

As Abraham saw the dry, lifeless wilderness that surrounded him, he had to be thinking, "Really, God? Are You sure this is the right way? Why did You bring me here?" There are times in life when we end up in places that feel exactly like that. Lonely desert wastelands that don't look very hopeful. It's easy in those times to question God and His plan.

In the Hebrew language, the word for "desert" is *midbar* (רבדמ). It means wilderness, desert, dry place. The Hebrew word for "speak" is *medaber* (רבדמ). Since Hebrew is spelled without vowels, the words are written exactly the same. Spoken differently, spelled the same. God wanted to *medaber* (speak) to Abraham, so He took him into the *midbar* (the wilderness), away from the noise and distractions.

When you study the Bible, you see that many times when God wanted to speak to His people, He called them out of the noise and regular cadence of life to a deserted, quiet place. He spoke to Moses on the backside of a mountain through a burning bush. He brought the Israelites out of Egypt into the wilderness to speak to them at Mount Sinai. He met with the prophets Elijah and Elisha in the wilderness. David wrote many of the psalms in the desert. Even Jesus, before He started His public ministry, was led by the Holy Spirit into the wilderness for forty days and nights to prepare Him for His purpose.

Whenever God calls you into a desert place, it's not to punish you, it's to prepare you.

So often when we end up in a barren place, we think it's punishment. "God, why have You left me here?" "Why have You abandoned me?" He hasn't left you there. He wants to speak to you there.

The wilderness is a place of separation.

Just as God had to separate Abraham from some of the ungodly influences in his life so He could speak to him and shape his future, God will call us to a place of separation that allows Him to speak into our lives. The wilderness removes us from some of the distractions that keep us from knowing and following God.

The place of separation becomes a place of preparation.

God uses the desert place to prepare us to trust Him when everything around us fails. It's there we learn to rely on His strength and provision instead of our own.

The place of separation becomes a place of revelation.

When God has our full attention, He can speak clearly to us. It's in those moments of desperation that God reveals Himself to us in new ways. We walk out of the wilderness experience with a renewed understanding of His power and care. We begin to see that He really is working all things together for our good. It's nearly impossible to get that revelation any other way.

Years ago, when we were walking through that desert place with our son, it felt like a place of separation. It pulled me away from my regularly scheduled, busy life. It arrested my attention. It brought me to my knees, and it became a place of revelation. During that time God convicted me about my tendency to be self-reliant and in control. By putting me in a situation that was completely out of my control, He helped me see my unhealthy need for control and how it usurps His rightful place in my life.

In this place of separation, God spoke to me about my empathy for others—or the lack of it. Up to that point I thought I was a fairly empathetic person who cared for the people around me. I was always willing to lend a helping hand or spend time praying with someone in need. But God showed me just how far I had to go—how self-focused I truly was.

The journey I've been on with my son has forever changed who I am as a father, a husband, a pastor, and a friend. It has changed how I see others. It has stirred a deeper compassion for those who are suffering in silence, struggling with life or faith or hope. And the longer I stay on this journey, the more God reveals how far I have to go.

But ultimately the place of separation gave me a greater revelation of God. When I grew quiet enough and stopped shouting my prayers on the back porch, I heard it. I heard the whisper of God.

THE WHISPER IN THE WIND

For several months Jefferson was rarely able to leave the house, which meant Julie was rarely able to leave the house. But after several weeks of being cooped up inside, we decided to take Jefferson and our dog, Sugar, to the beach to get outside to walk and pray. I remember Jefferson walking with Sugar just a few feet ahead of us. Julie and I were walking behind him praying and crying. It was in the middle of the darkest days, and we were losing our boy.

For weeks we had been to doctors. For weeks we had been rehearsing the bad reports. What will happen if nothing changes? Will Jefferson be able to function on his own? He's an only child. What kind of future could he possibly have?

As those thoughts rumbled through our head, a guy came walking toward us on the beach. Normally I would never encourage anyone to get their theology from a T-shirt on the beach in South Florida. That could be very dangerous. But that day the Lord brought a man wearing a T-shirt across our path. Printed on the shirt in bold letters were the words "Listen to what you know—NOT to what you fear." It was as if the voice of God whispered to me and repeated what I had just read: "Todd, listen to what you know, not to what you fear."

Immediately Julie and I realized we had been listening to the voice of fear. We had been rehearsing the words that fear were speaking over our son, and it only produced anxiety and worry in our hearts and minds. Our negative self-talk had caused us to doubt that anything would change. We were verbally playing out the worst-case scenario— speaking words of doubt that were fueling our fears. But that day on the beach, away from the noise, we heard the whisper of the Holy Spirit.

In order to *listen* to what we know, somebody had to be *speaking* it, so we began to declare the truth of God out loud to each other every day. We read the Word of God over ourselves and over Jefferson, reminding us of God's promises. What we *did* know about God is that

- He is faithful (Ps. 36:5).

- He is able to do more than we could ever hope, think, or imagine (Eph. 3:20).

- He is Jehovah-Rapha, the God who heals (*present tense*, Exod. 15:26).

- He who began a good work in Jefferson is faithful to complete it (Phil. 1:6).

- He is a good, good Father, and He has planned a hope and a future for our son (Jer. 29:11).

- The One who is the same yesterday, today, and forever is already waiting for Jefferson in his future (Heb. 13:8).

We began to declare what we knew to be true. We replaced the words of worry and fear with declarations of faith. And we did this every day, even when we didn't feel like it. *Especially* when we didn't feel like it. We put scriptures on sticky notes all around the house, words that declared who Jefferson was and the big future God had for him. Nothing changed that day, but something shifted on the inside of us. Slowly, our faith grew, and what had shifted on the inside began to shift things on the outside. The atmosphere in our home changed. Faith was on the rise. Hope returned to our hearts. Our declarations of faith began to silence the doubt.

I'd like to say we came home from the beach that day and within a couple of weeks of declaring Scripture over Jefferson, he was healthy and healed, but it didn't happen that way. Remember I said we were on the *journey plan* for our miracle, and on a long journey it's easy to miss the small wonders God is working out. You have to keep your spiritual eyes open.

Right after our encounter on the beach, Julie decided it was time to get Jefferson back in church. Large crowds had been overwhelming, so he hadn't been to church for months. Julie took him to middle school student night, and the two of them sat alone at the very back of the auditorium. The band

> **Listen to what you know—not to what you fear.**

started to play and all the students ran to the front to worship. Jefferson just sat on the back row, alone with his mom. Then three middle school boys ran up to where they were seated, grabbed Jefferson by the arm, and said, "You're coming with us." Julie watched as Jefferson gradually engaged with the students down front. One hand went up, then both as he joined in the praise and worship. As she watched, she heard the whisper. God spoke to her and said, "This spiritual home and family that you and Todd are building for everyone else, it's for your family too. It's for Jefferson. You can't give him everything he needs, but I can."

We have spent our lives building Christ Fellowship, creating a spiritual home for people. We often say that church isn't a building you go into, it's a family you belong to. In the days that followed we saw Jefferson being loved and cared for by his church family in extraordinary ways. Mentors and friends spoke life over him. They built faith and confidence back in him. People took him by the hand and said, "Jefferson, you're coming with us," and they pulled him out of the emotional hole he was in.

It took another eighteen months of holding on to the

promises of God until we saw the clouds begin to part and joy and life come back to our son. And while we are still holding on to those promises, we've witnessed God come through in remarkable ways.

Jefferson started playing guitar and joined a local theater group. He began to break out of his shell and make new friends. He got into a small group at church and began to grow in his relationship with God and with the other students. Within the next few years, he graduated high school and went on to graduate from Southeastern University at the top of his class! In 2020, as if nothing else was happening, he married the girl of his dreams, Cassie, whom he met while serving at church. Today Jefferson is a worship leader pouring into the next generation of students at Christ Fellowship. And while his story is still being written, we continue to make declarations of faith over his future. We learned that seasons of silence must be filled with words of faith. And those declarations of faith can unlock destinies.

WORK OUT THE DOUBT

1. Is there an area you are praying for in which it seems like God is silent?

2. How can you "listen to what you know, not what you fear"? (Use Appendix B if necessary.)

What I fear:

What I know:

What I fear:

What I know:

Chapter 11

WHEN DOUBT LEADS TO FAITH

Faith does not eliminate questions. But
faith knows where to take them.
—Elisabeth Elliot

THE 2004 HURRICANE season was brutal on Florida. Four major hurricanes hit our state. Two of those storms tore across South Florida, where we live, uprooting trees, destroying buildings, and leaving us without power for three weeks. During one hurricane I recall looking out a window as the storm passed by. Debris was flying through the air, and the palm trees in the yard were being pulled from one side to the other. It looked as if they would snap from 130 mph winds.

After the storm we spent weeks cleaning up our community. Many people lost portions of their roof and had major tree damage. Our yard looked like a bomb had gone off; branches and debris were everywhere. Two large trees over forty feet tall were completely uprooted, lying on their sides. But I noticed not one palm tree was destroyed. They had lost some branches, and the ones still attached looked like they had been through World War III, but the palm trees were all still standing tall. A landscaper told me it's because their trunks are woodless and flexible. Their roots spread out like a carpet, giving them balance.

He informed me that palm trees actually grow stronger after a storm.

The landscaper was right. Scientists have discovered that when a palm tree experiences hurricane-force winds, its roots grow stronger. The stress of strong winds stimulates palms to strengthen their root systems. The stress prompts the roots to grow deeper to maintain stability. This adaptive growth response ensures that palms are not only able to survive future storms, but they actually become more resilient over time.[1] The storm makes them stronger.

When I look back at the storms I've weathered that challenged my faith—the storms with Jefferson, the storms in leadership—I can see now that God used them for my good. At the time, there was nothing "good" about them, but in the rearview mirror I can discern the benefit of doubt, the benefit of a newfound resilience, a clearer perspective, and a strengthened faith that has only grown over time and under pressure. The same kind of pressure the palm tree endures during the storm.

Often, when we look back at a challenging season of life, we get a clearer perspective. In the middle of the storm you're holding on for life, just hoping to make it through, but once the storm is over and the clouds have parted, you realize you've come through stronger, more resilient. That's what I discovered. Without my realizing it, my doubt had strengthened my faith.

DOUBT: AN UNLIKELY ALLY

Theologian Paul Tillich famously said, "Doubt is not the opposite of faith; it is an element of faith."[2] Questioning and uncertainty are not only natural but necessary for a dynamic and robust faith. Healthy doubt means we're thinking. Processing. Seeking to understand. It means you're asking questions. Why do I believe what I believe? What is at the foundation of my faith? Doubt is not a departure from faith but a journey within it. It compels a believer to dive deeper into the reasons behind their beliefs and seek answers that satisfy their intellectual and spiritual uncertainty.

In the middle of my doubt, when I was questioning what I believed (and what I was preaching on Sundays), it forced the questions I never had the courage to ask before. It drove me to the Word of God to better understand the context of some of the promises I was holding on to. Were they reliable? Could they be an anchor for me in this storm, or was I holding on to a pool floatie that was quickly losing air?

> **Without my realizing it, my doubt had strengthened my faith.**

Doubt drove me to seek out trusted advisers, men and women who had walked with God much longer than I had. I needed their godly insight to the Scriptures and the questions I had. Doubt drove me to my knees. I prayed like I had never prayed before. I was desperate for God. And when I resurfaced at the end of my hurricane with doubt, I found myself stronger, like the palm tree. My spiritual roots had grown deeper during the storm. Without my realizing it, every prayer, every spiritual conversation, every question of doubt had strengthened my faith.

UNHEALTHY DOUBT

Not everyone who battles with doubt will emerge with stronger faith. The result is determined by how a person processes their doubt. Healthy doubt seeks to find truth. It wants to understand. It is an authentic pursuit of what is real and reliable. I believe most people fall into this category. When it comes to faith in God, there is a desire in the heart of every person to know Him. We've been created with this longing by our Creator, for our Creator. And while this may be our innate desire or *intention*, how we deal with doubt will determine our *direction*. Life's challenges can drive us toward a healthy pursuit of God or lead us down the path of unhealthy doubt.

Unhealthy or unproductive doubt is often wrapped in pain and disappointment that can push a person away from faith and away from God. This pain could come from one of the catalysts of doubt we discussed, where God did not come through the way we thought He would. But often this pain is caused by a person. And when that person is associated with God, either as part of a faith community or even someone who "works for God," it's difficult to separate that pain from God. I would never want to downplay or dismiss when someone has been hurt by a person in the church, but that hurt did not come from God. That was not God, and it wasn't "the church." It was a person who claims to be a Christian that did something un-Christlike.

Remember, there is no such thing as a perfect church. I often tell our congregation that if they ever find the perfect church, they better not join it, or they will mess it up—and so would I. The church is made up of imperfect people trying to love and follow God better every day.

But the imperfect people in the church don't negate the God-ordained, perfect purpose that is *on* the church. The church is God's perfect plan for you to find a place in His family, a place of community and spiritual growth. The enemy's plan is to get you isolated from the place that can strengthen your walk with God, and he will do anything he can, use *anyone* he can, to cause you to doubt God and walk away from your faith.

When we're dealing with unhealthy doubt, we build a case for all the reasons to stay away from God and remain in our disbelief. Unhealthy doubt works to find excuses for not trusting God and walking away from faith. You know a person is entertaining unhealthy doubt when cynical declarations outnumber honest questions, when proving a point is more important than discovering the truth. Anytime we battle with doubt, our tendency will be to justify our perspective. Explain our apprehensions. Defend our doubt. Responding this way will keep us stuck and stunted in our spiritual growth. There is a more productive way forward that leads to reaping the benefits available to us.

Fruit in Every Season

"The righteous shall flourish like a palm tree, he shall grow like a cedar in Lebanon. Those who are planted in the house of the LORD shall flourish in the courts of our God. They shall still bear fruit in old age; they shall be fresh and flourishing" (Ps. 92:12–14, NKJV).

That word *flourish* means to thrive, grow strong, bear fruit. God wants your life to flourish in every season, even the most challenging ones you face. Scholars believe King

David wrote Psalm 92 to declare that God is trustworthy, faithful to His promises. This was the man who experienced many doubts and delays on his journey of faith. Here he gives us insight into coming through those battles stronger.

David compares us, those made righteous in Christ, to a palm tree. We've already discovered that palm trees can not only survive storms and hurricanes but come through them stronger. Their roots grow deeper. Palm trees can also survive in nearly any condition. Palm trees grow in the desert. In Florida we have palm trees lining our beaches, where there's nothing but sand. Still, they grow tall and produce fruit.

David also says we will be like the cedars of Lebanon. These trees are mentioned several times in Scripture and are noted for their strength. Some cedar trees can grow to be over 130 feet tall. Their roots go down deep and wrap around underground rock for stability. They are known for their longevity. Some cedars are over two thousand years old and still bearing fruit. If a tree has lived two thousand years, you know it has experienced some storms and weathered some droughts.

This passage is a picture of the life God has for you, no matter what storms you will go through. The storms of doubt and the seasons of drought will not take you out. You can make it through those seasons when it feels as if God is absent and His voice is silent. You can still be growing strong and bearing much fruit.

But the only way you will flourish is found in the second part of that passage. It would be difficult, if not impossible, for you to thrive without it. Right after David says, "The righteous shall flourish like a palm tree, he shall grow like a cedar in Lebanon" (v. 12), he says, "Those who are planted in the house of the LORD shall flourish in the courts of our God" (v. 13). You have to be planted to get in on the promise.

Planted Versus Potted

Planted, by definition, means to put something firmly in a particular place. For a seed to grow, it must get planted. A seed has all the potential to become a fruit-producing, oxygen-generating life source, but it has to get *planted* to reach its potential. If it stays in a bag, on a shelf, it will never flourish. It will never become what it was created to be.

Too many people are potted and never get planted. A potted plant can't reach its potential either. It's limited. It depends on someone else to water it and care for it. When the storms come, the potted plant is toppled over or blown away. It can't put down roots.

Have you ever bought a plant at a nursery, taken it home to plant it, and discovered when you took it out of the container that there was hardly any dirt? Just a big bundle of roots. The plant was root-bound. Its growth had been limited by the container it was in. Too many of us get limited and our faith can't grow. So when the storm comes and we face doubts and questions about God, we topple over. Get blown away. But when we are planted and our roots can go down deep, finding their own source of nutrients, we're no longer impacted by what's happening around us.

> But blessed is the one who trusts in the LORD, whose
> confidence is in him. They will be like a tree planted
> by the water that sends out its roots by the stream. It

does not fear when heat comes; its leaves are always green. It has no worries in a year of drought and never fails to bear fruit.

—JEREMIAH 17:7-8, NIV

The tree planted by the water is a life deeply connected to the source of spiritual nourishment—God Himself. When we trust in God, our faith is like that tree with roots reaching deep into the stream, drawing life and strength even in times of drought and doubt. Our faith is anchored to God

> You have to be planted to get in on the promise.

and His promises, not to our changing circumstances and feelings. And the promise is that you will always bear fruit. Your life will produce life for others. So stay planted in God's Word. It is the light for your path when you face dark seasons of doubt. Stay planted in God's house where there are people who will feed your faith and help you grow.

Maybe you've come through some storms of doubt and it feels like your life has been uprooted. You haven't weathered it like those palm trees. You look more like the tree in my yard after the hurricane, lying on its side, branches broken. Or the potted plant that's been tossed around in the storm. If that's you, I understand. I was there too. But I learned that doubt doesn't have to be the end of your faith. It can be the catalyst to a deeper, more intimate relationship with God and the people He has put in your life. Here's what I discovered:

Desperation deepens your connection with God.

Desperation drives you to your knees. When we come to the end of ourselves and what we can do, it forces us to hold on to God. Jeremiah 29:13 (NIV) promises, "You will seek me and find me when you seek me with all your heart." I've personally come to know God and the work of the Holy Spirit in a more profound way as a result of my battle with doubt. My desperate search for the answers to my questions led me to a deeper knowledge of God. I've discovered that when you run to God, you will ultimately find Him.

Doubts can lead to deeper community.

As you open up and share your struggle within a healthy faith community, it will strengthen the connection between you and the people God has placed in your life. Their prayers and faith will carry you. The Bible tells us that we have been created to be the answer to one another's prayers. There are some things you are asking from God that He wants to give you through His people. Your humility and authenticity in these moments remove the barriers and allow for a deeper connection with your spiritual family. When I shared my doubts with the people in my life, it took our relationship deeper. They knew I was trusting them with something very fragile, and that trust took our friendship to another level.

Doubt can make your faith believable.

Just as fire refines gold, doubt can refine your faith by burning away superficial beliefs you've accepted without knowing why. Your doubt can lead to a deeper understanding of God and His truth. When you know *why* you believe *what* you believe, your faith becomes believable; it becomes a solid foundation you can build your life upon. I came through my struggle with doubt with a greater grasp on what I believed and who my God is. My doubt strengthened my faith.

Doubt is not an obstacle to faith but a vital component of our spiritual journey. It challenges us to deepen our understanding of God's Word and His ways. It creates more authentic connection within our faith community. And doubt can lead us into a more intimate relationship with our Creator. By staying rooted in God—through Scripture, prayer, community, and worship—we can navigate our doubts to deepen our trust in God and strengthen our faith.

WORK OUT THE DOUBT

1. What are the key differences between healthy doubt and unhealthy doubt?

   Healthy Doubt:

   Unhealthy Doubt:

2. Think of a time when doubt strengthened your faith. What did you do to turn your doubt into faith?

3. Who is the person you can turn to in times of doubt to help strengthen your faith? How do they do this?

Part III

DOUBTING
OTHERS

Chapter 12

WHEN DOUBT TAKES OUT A RELATIONSHIP

It is not an enemy who taunts me—I could bear that. It is not my foes who so arrogantly insult me—I could have hidden from them. Instead, it is you—my equal, my companion and close friend. What good fellowship we once enjoyed as we walked together to the house of God.
—PSALM 55:12–14

H E WAS ONE of my closest friends. More like a brother. We worked in ministry together. Our families vacationed together. At times we were inseparable. Then one day everything changed. I remember the moment he asked me not to call him anymore. He said he needed space and didn't want to talk. I was obviously hurt. Confused. In fact, to this day I still don't understand what was so terrible that we couldn't restore the relationship, though I do know we both had a part to play in the friendship falling apart.

As I look back, I see now how doubt played a role in disrupting our relationship. Doubting the other person's motives. Questioning their intentions. Doubting if they were being completely honest with what they said. It all cast a shadow of doubt over our friendship, and that shadow showed up in future relationships in the form of distance and suspicion, afraid of getting burned again.

We all experience hurts and disappointments from people in our lives. It's an inevitable part of being in a relationship. Sometimes the pain comes from those closest to us—friends, family members, or coworkers—people we trust and rely on. When these individuals hurt us, our natural tendency is to withdraw. We question their love, loyalty, and intentions, allowing doubt to erode the relationship.

Betrayal from a friend is one of the most profound forms of hurt we will ever experience. It strikes at the core of our trust and leaves lasting scars. Dr. John Gottman is a relationship researcher who warns that betrayal can take many forms, including infidelity, dishonesty, and broken promises. "Betrayal in a relationship can create a profound sense of loss and disillusionment. It shakes the foundation of trust and can lead to feelings of anger, sadness, and confusion."[1] At one point in our lives all of us have been betrayed by someone we care about. In fact, there's a good chance that person came to mind as you were reading these words.

THE REVELATION OF EXPECTATION

Expectations play a significant role in how we perceive hurt and disappointment. When the expectations of others are not met, we feel let down and sometimes betrayed. The problem is that so many of our expectations are *unspoken* or *unexamined*. Unspoken expectations assume the other person should know or will figure out what you need from the relationship without you having to say it.

Sounds unfair, even unreasonable. Unexamined expectations are demands we put on a person without evaluating if they are even possible. Can they even give us what we are expecting from them? Unexamined expectations place unrealistic demands on the other person, leaving us open to no other outcome but disappointment.

It wasn't until doubt found its way into some of my relationships, specifically the close friendship that ended abruptly, that I realized I had put unreasonable and unspoken expectations on several of the people in my life. There were things I *assumed* they knew I needed from them. An unwritten code of conduct. Issues I expected them to care about as much as I did. Basic rules of engagement that friendships are built upon. *But we never talked about any of these.* I just assumed they were universally understood.

This revelation forced me to examine all my relationships. Where was I living with unspoken or unexamined expectations? What unreasonable demands had I put on my wife, on my son, on my parents, or on the team I was leading? It caused me to question if the relationship dysfunction I was experiencing was primarily my fault. Where had I allowed unmet expectations to lead to a fracture in a friendship, which had caused me to withdraw and hold back from the people in my life? I realized I was the common denominator in all my relationships, so if I got better, I was guaranteed my relationships would at least get 50 percent better.

When we experience hurt or betrayal in a relationship, our instinct is to pull back and protect ourselves. We want to avoid further pain. This often displays itself as emotional distancing, avoiding the other person in social settings or building walls around our heart. We've all heard the adage "Hurt me once, shame on you. Hurt me twice, shame on me." But that mindset creates a culture of suspicion, looking for the other person to let us down—again.

When we doubt other people's motives and question their sincerity, it creates a cycle of skepticism and mistrust that makes it difficult to maintain healthy relationships. Social psychologists have determined that negative experiences in our life have the tendency to impact us more than positive ones. Psychologists believe "our brains are wired to pay more attention to negative experiences and threats, which can lead to a heightened sense of mistrust and doubt."[2] This ultimately throws us in a cycle of mistrust with the people in our lives. We live from the defensive position with the expectation that someone else will let us down.

When Doubt Leads to Isolation

When that close friendship broke years ago, I remember my first response was shock and disbelief, followed closely by emotional withdrawal. I didn't want to go through this again with another friend, so I gradually put up walls. Not high walls to keep everyone out, but high enough to keep anyone from getting *that* close again. Without realizing it, I was allowing doubt to take me out of the friend game. I was allowing the pain from this one relationship to negatively impact all my relationships, and as a result I was heading toward isolation. When we put up walls, they can keep out the bad—the pain and feelings of betrayal—but they also keep out the good, the joy and connection that only come through deep, personal relationships.

Withdrawing from people might give us temporary relief from pain, but it usually leads to the greater injuries of isolation and loneliness, affecting our emotional and physical well-being. I remember the months following this failed friendship; I struggled with depression for the first time in my life. I'm normally a very positive person. They say some people see the glass as half empty, while others see the glass half full. I usually see the glass as overflowing, so

> When we put up walls, they can keep out the bad—the pain and feelings of betrayal—but they also keep out the good.

for me to lose my joy and struggle with depression was new territory. I didn't know how to deal with this type of discouragement and doubt. I found myself questioning other relationships in my life, fearing more disappointment was inevitable. My fears were running wild. I should have recognized something was wrong and needed my attention.

DOUBT ON YOUR DASHBOARD

Julie's Volvo is about eight years old. It's been a great car for our family, and it still has a few good years left on it. But when you've had a car that long it develops some character flaws (usually right after the warranty runs out). The window that doesn't roll down all the way, or the cigarette lighter that doesn't charge your phone any longer. Julie's car has a light on her dashboard that will randomly come on. It's a little symbol that looks like a flat tire, and the car's computer tells her to "check tire pressure."

The first time this happened, we immediately pulled the car over and checked the tires. Everything looked OK, but just to make sure we drove it to the dealership. Nothing was wrong. It was a computer glitch. The technician reset the computer and off we went. A couple of months later it happened again. Once again we pulled over, checked the tires, and all of them looked fine. This time we didn't bother going back to the dealership; it was too much of a hassle. It probably was just the computer again.

This happened a few more times over the next few months. When the car went in for its next checkup, the technician confirmed it was just a computer issue and told us how much it would cost to fix it. The amount was more than my first car cost me, so we passed. We learned to live with a little warning light that randomly came on.

But recently it happened again. Julie noticed the warning light and didn't give it a thought. She kept driving, running her errands and heading into work. Later that day someone stopped by her office to tell her that her tire was completely flat. She had been driving around with a flat tire. She had been so distracted that day she didn't notice the car wasn't handling properly. If she had gotten on the interstate with that flat tire, it could have been catastrophic.

I believe many of us have a warning light going off in our lives, but we've gotten so used to it that we've become desensitized. We've learned to live with it, and we don't do anything about it because it feels *complicated* or *costly*. We've tried to fix it before, but it just keeps coming back on. We don't realize the tire is flat and we're headed for danger.

The Epidemic of Loneliness

This dilemma is so serious that the US Surgeon General issued a warning about it. Dr. Vivek Murthy published a report in 2023 titled "Our Epidemic of Loneliness and Isolation," in which he states that loneliness is the single largest threat to our physical and mental well-being. The Surgeon General went on to say that isolation and loneliness are more dangerous than diabetes or obesity, and he compared the impact to smoking fifteen cigarettes a day![3]

A recent survey reported that nearly two-thirds of people anonymously admitted to being lonely. Two-thirds! That's the majority of the people you work with, go to church with, or hang out with. The report went on to say that only 12 percent of them would admit it publicly. People see loneliness as a weakness or something to be ashamed of.[4]

Isolation has become our hidden epidemic, removing us from one of life's greatest pleasures and necessities. God created us for relationship. Genesis declares that we have been made in the image of God, and our God is a relational God. The Trinity is relational. God the Father, God the Son, and God the Holy Spirit. Three in one. They are never separated or alone.

In Genesis, when God created the heavens and the earth, He declared, "It is good." When He created the birds of the air and the beasts of the fields, again He said, "It is good." In fact, the first thing that God declared "not good" wasn't sin or disobedience or the devil. It was *isolation*. "It is not good for the man to be alone" (Gen. 2:18). Isolation disrupts God's plan for your life. It segments you away from the very thing God created you for: life-giving relationships. If you are lonely, it's not because there is something *wrong* with you; it's what's *right* with you. There is a problem that you know needs to be fixed.

Many of us have the warning light on the dashboard. Maybe it's been there so long we've learned to live with it. We mentioned earlier that doubt can serve as a warning indicator, letting us know there's a problem that needs to be addressed. It's the light on the dashboard telling you to check your tire pressure or oil level, telling you it's time to stop and refuel or you'll end up on the side of road in life, stranded and alone.

> God created us
> for relationship.

ASKING FOR HELP

Sometimes when the light comes on, you're not sure what to do. That was my story. I had never been down this road before. I wasn't used to dealing with this type of relationship doubt and discouragement. I remember sharing my struggle with Julie, not that she hadn't already observed it. It was obvious. We had talked about the situation for several weeks leading up to this conversation, but this was different. I needed her help. I let her know just how disheartened I had become.

Pulling back the curtain gave her a greater understanding of what was going on inside my heart and mind. It gave her freedom to speak specifically to the lies I was believing. She prayed with me. She prayed the Scriptures over me, and she encouraged me to talk with my parents and to our friend Lance Witt, a trusted friend and pastor who has helped us process life and leadership for nearly two decades.

After a few conversations I decided to open up with a few more close friends and with the team I was leading at church. I wanted them to know what I was going through and how to pray for me. Being vulnerable with them was one of the hardest things I had to do.

As a leader you're trained to believe you have to have it all together. You have to be the one with the answers. You can't be seen as weak, and I saw vulnerability as a weakness. But I soon discovered that vulnerability isn't a weakness—it's a strength. It was the starting point for change, for healing, for finding what I was searching for. As I became transparent about what I was experiencing, I began breaking down the walls of isolation and opening myself up to more authentic and meaningful relationships. Sharing what I was going through gave the people around me a greater insight to what I needed as a friend. It gave them permission to go there with me. To walk with me. Pray for me. It became the way others helped me find my way forward.

RELATIONSHIPS REQUIRED

Looking back, I realized that I needed people to help me move past the pain caused by people. I had to be open and vulnerable in order to heal. It's ironic that the very thing that caused me pain in the first place was the prescription for my recovery. Relationships are required.

Relationships are a requirement of life. Like air is to the lungs and food is to the body, so relationships are to our soul and development. Without relationships it is impossible to become the person God created you to be. They not only bring fulfillment and joy to our lives, but they are also tools in the hands of God to refine our character and shape our personality. We can never learn to be selfless apart from people. We will never learn how to pray for our enemy if we isolate ourselves from our enemies. God uses people to form our person, to make us more like Jesus.

In fact, there are fifty-nine instructions in the New Testament that you cannot fulfill apart from people. Fifty-nine "one another" scriptures. Love one another (Rom. 13:8). Forgive one another as Christ forgave you (Eph. 4:32). Live in harmony with one another (Rom. 12:16). It's easy to live in harmony when there's nobody around to disagree with you. It is in the challenging situations of real life that our lives not only take on meaning but they are formed into the likeness of Christ.

This is why it is critically important for you to deal with doubt when it comes to your relationships. Take the first step. Have the hard conversation. Push past the awkward differences. If you don't, you'll go through life disconnected from the people God has purposefully placed in it.

PROCEED WITH CAUTION

I know it's risky. There's a certainty you will be hurt again. Someone will let you down. But don't let that stop you. Don't let doubt or disappointment take you out of the relationship game. I've learned a lot about friendships over these past few years. Relationships should come with a warning label: "DANGER. Handle carefully. High Risk of Injury or Death." (OK, maybe that last one is a bit melodramatic.) But relationship pain is *real*. And learning how to deal with it is *really* important.

As a pastor, I've had the privilege and responsibility to

be with people as they are getting ready to step into eternity. One thing I can assure you of is that nobody who's getting ready to take their final breath is worried about the stock market. They're not worried about politics or the price of eggs. The only thing they care about is their relationships. Specifically, their relationship with God—Do they have one? Because they are getting ready to meet Him—and their relationships with their family and friends. It's the only thing that counts.

> God uses people to form our person, to make us more like Jesus.

So if the meaning of life comes down to the quality of your relationships, wouldn't it be vital that you don't allow anything to rob you of the only thing that matters? Wouldn't it be worth the time and energy to learn the enemy's strategy to take out your relationships and build a defense plan that protects what's most valuable? When it comes to your relationships, don't let doubt take you out.

WORK OUT THE DOUBT

1. Have you ever felt betrayed in a relationship or friendship? How did that impact your trust in others?

2. How does isolation only make our problem worse?

3. What should you do if your "warning light of loneliness" is alerting you that something is off?

Chapter 13

PEACEMAKER VERSUS PEACE FAKER

Blessed are the peacemakers, for they
will be called children of God.
—MATTHEW 5:9, NIV

SEVERAL YEARS AGO Julie and I were traveling overseas and hadn't been able to watch the news for nearly a week. We arrived in Italy and noticed soldiers lining the streets, automatic rifles in hand. There were hundreds of them, standing in front of barricades, blocking access to certain roads. We assumed there must have been an international incident or threat we were unaware of. We asked our guide about the military presence and if there was anything we needed to be concerned about. He looked back at us and casually said, "No, they're just here to keep the peace." The same soldiers who had been trained for battle were there to keep the peace. The same training required to go to war was required to keep the peace.

We have this misconception that peacemakers are passive, that in order to keep the peace in a relationship you must put up with another person's unreasonable behavior. To be a peacemaker you have to keep your mouth shut and let the other person have their way. But the reality is that peacemakers are not passive. They have to be skilled soldiers, fighting for peace.

BATTLE READY

When doubt tries to take out the relationship, ruin the friendship, or destroy the marriage, it will attack as a skilled warrior. Doubt and suspicion fight side by side, making you question the other person's loyalty and commitment. And if doubt wins, trust and intimacy are the casualties, and you're left feeling isolated and detached. Without a battle plan you won't be able to take out this enemy.

The Bible is full of fighting words when it comes to peace. Ephesians 4:3 (NIV) says, "Make every effort to keep

> The same training required to go to war was required to keep the peace.

the unity of the spirit through the bond of peace." That phrase "every effort" means you don't give up. You won't back down. You are going to fight for the relationship. Hebrews 12:14 (AMPC) tells us to "strive to live in peace with everybody." That word *strive* in the original language means to chase after or hunt down. Peace is hard work.

One of the guarantees of any relationship is conflict. I remember when Julie and I were in premarital counseling. My father was our pastor, so he was preparing us for marriage. In one of our sessions we were talking about conflict. He told us that when we get into an argument we should stop and pray together. Up to that point Julie and I had not had any real arguments. Rarely a disagreement.

I sat in my dad's office that day thinking to myself, "I'm never going to fight with Julie. She's my pookie. I love my pookie." But it wasn't too long before pookie was on my last nerve.

Our first argument actually took place on our honeymoon. (Of course, we both tell this story from slightly different perspectives, but since this is my book, you get to hear my side of it.) We were leaving a parking garage in Charleston, South Carolina, and I couldn't find the parking ticket. Cars were piling up behind us. The parking garage attendant looked frustrated, and I was in a bit of a panic. I looked over and saw Julie glancing in the mirror, putting on lipstick, completely unaware of the situation. My frustration came through in my voice when I asked her, "Would you help me find the ticket?" Now, to be fair, when she tells this story she says my voice had a low, guttural, demonic sound. I don't remember it that way, but I do remember the hours of deafening silence that followed.

Looking back on that story we both can laugh now, but in the moment it brought conflict into our relationship. Conflict that created a separation. When conflict enters a relationship, it can cause you to doubt the other person and their intentions. It can make you question their love and commitment. It plants the seeds of doubt that cause you to ask why they reacted that way—why they treated you that way. The seeds are planted, and they begin to grow.

The reason I'm dedicating a chapter to this issue is because most of us were never equipped to handle conflict in our relationships. I don't recall one class in high school or college dedicated to conflict resolution, but it's a skill we all need to master. If conflict goes unchecked or unresolved, it has the potential to destroy a friendship, a work environment, or a family unit. Conflict itself isn't bad, but unresolved conflict can erode the foundations of a relationship, opening the door for doubt. Doubt and suspicion are often the subtle intruders. They sneak into our hearts and minds, often unnoticed at first, but over time they can become barriers between us and those we love.

Fighters and Fleers

In all my years of pastoring and counseling I've discovered there are two types of people: *fighters* and *fleers*. Those who want to fight it out and those who run at the first sign of conflict. And many times in a marriage, one spouse is the fighter while the other is the fleer. Julie is the fleer (although I must say she's gotten much better with conflict being married to me). That day on our honeymoon, she was sitting in the car, holding her tongue, thinking she was the picture of a peacemaker. If there was a picture in the Bible next to Matthew 5:9, "Blessed are the peacemakers," it would be a picture of Julie. *But* there's a difference between being a peacemaker and a peace faker.

Peace fakers are passive, hoping their silence or lack of engagement in the discussion will create peace. But instead, it usually creates a big gap in the relationship, as it did that day on our honeymoon—which is not what you want happening on your honeymoon. Peace fakers hope peace will happen. Peacemakers *make* peace happen. They take the initiative. Jesus said, "Blessed are the peacemakers, for they will be called children of God" (Matt. 5:9, NIV). Peacemakers are called the children of God because children can't help but reflect and resemble their parents, and our heavenly Father is the ultimate Peacemaker. From the very beginning God has run toward conflict and brokenness. He always makes the first move, doing whatever is necessary to make peace. He goes so far as to give us His Son as a payment for sin so we can live at peace with Him. Peacemakers are like their Father.

For some of us, our upbringing makes us conflict avoidant—doing whatever we can to steer away from contention and strife. We grow up thinking that conflict is the absence of unity when conflict is actually the opportunity for unity. Conflict becomes the opportunity to love the other person completely, the opportunity to honor them even when you can't understand where they're coming from. It's the opportunity to invite Christ into the middle of the mess—to not allow the problem to become more important than the person.

When handled correctly, conflict becomes an opportunity for the relationship to grow. Research has found that people who engage in open, honest conversation during times of disagreement and conflict report they are happier and more satisfied with the relationship.[1] The same study reported that avoiding or suppressing conflict leads to negative feelings of resentment and emotional distance.

> **We grow up thinking that conflict is the absence of unity when conflict is actually the opportunity for unity.**

One study found that healthy conflict resolution isn't just good for the relationship, it's good for the individuals. When you take the time to work through what's causing the break in the relationship, it produces lower levels of anxiety and increased emotional stability and overall happiness.[2] But we don't need a clinical report to tell us that. We've all experienced the strain on the relationship and our emotional health when conflict goes unresolved. Our minds try to make sense of what happened and often create distorted scenarios. I've personally experienced the crippling effect of unresolved conflict.

Life is all about relationships. When your relationships are good, life is good. But when your relationships are bad, life is bad. It doesn't matter how much money you have or how much success you've experienced, when your relationships are messed up, all of life feels messed up. And many times that is because we haven't learned to resolve conflict, so we open the door for doubt to build mistrust in the relationship.

RESOLUTION OR RECONCILIATION

There is a difference between resolution and reconciliation. Resolving the disagreement and bringing clarity to the issue is much different from reconciling the relationship. One is focused on the problem, the other on the person. One is consumed with making sure everyone agrees and acknowledges who was right in the argument, while the other is willing to let the issue go unresolved so the relationship can heal.

Many times I've gotten this wrong. I found myself in a disagreement with someone, and I was more concerned with proving my point than protecting the friendship. I wanted the other person to understand my perspective and ultimately recognize I was right. Even if I was the first to apologize, my "apology" was often crafted to reinforce my position. In the end I may have won the argument, but I lost in the relationship.

In Matthew 5, right after Jesus says, "Blessed are the peacemakers," He goes on to say, "Therefore, if you are offering your gift at the altar and there remember that your brother or sister has something against you, leave your gift there in front of the altar. First go and be reconciled to them; then come and offer your gift" (vv. 23–24, NIV). Notice Jesus doesn't talk about resolving the issue or fixing the problem. He is all about fixing the relationship. Reconciliation is so important to Him that He says, "Don't waste your time worshipping God if you've got unreconciled relationships."

Later, when asked about the greatest commandment, Jesus directly connects our love for God to our love for each other. According to Jesus, you can't separate the two. Our God is a relational God, and He wants you to work hard for the relationship.

Do the Hard Work

As I shared before, I was never good at journaling until I was drowning in the crisis of Jefferson's health. I started writing down my thoughts and prayers, and it helped me process and pour out my heart to God.

One day as I was praying about a damaged friendship, I asked that God would heal the relationship, mend back together what had been torn apart. As I wrote the words onto the page of my journal, I heard the Holy Spirit whisper, "You do it. You heal the relationship." I was shocked. I thought that was God's job. I thought I had already done everything I could. I had forgiven this person and made several attempts to reconcile with them. I had reached out and left voice messages on their phone. But in prayer that day, the Holy Spirit told me to try again. To be a peacemaker. To do the hard work.

As I thought about what God was asking me to do, I made excuses. "This person doesn't want a relationship with me anymore. That ship has sailed. They probably wouldn't return my call even if I did reach out." Doubt was at work, trying to convince me it was hopeless, that I might as well give up on this relationship. Doubt was trying to rob me of obeying God. Make me think I knew better than God. It was trying to deprive me of the joy of a restored relationship.

It took me a few days to process the best way to reach out to this old friend, but when I did it was as if the walls began to crumble. Years of doubting each other's motive and questioning each other's comments seemed to fade. We were on the road back to restoring what had been broken.

In this situation, my attempt to heal the relationship was received well. The other person was open and ready to do the hard work of mending what was broken. But there have been many other fractured friendships that never healed. When I reached out to rekindle the relationship, I was met with resistance or unanswered phone calls. Those responses make us hesitant to try again. We're a little gun-shy. It's just easier not to do the hard work. But without giving it a go, you'll never know what you could have.

I wonder what relationship you've given up on. I wonder who it is in your life about whom God would say, "Heal the relationship. You do it." Like me, you may have tried more times than you can count. Doubt might tell you the same lies it told me, but when you step out in the grace and kindness of God, with a heart to reconcile the relationship even if the differences never get resolved, you'll be surprised at what God can do.

When it comes to reconciling relationships, there are a few lessons I learned that will help you take out doubt before it takes out the relationship.

Fight on Your Knees

You might expect a pastor to tell you to pray, but I don't say that as a spiritual platitude. The truth is *God can do more in seconds than man can do in centuries.* One of the greatest things you can do for any relationship you have is pray. When you do, you are inviting the presence of God into that friendship, that marriage, that business partnership. Even if the other person won't pray with you, you pray. Invite God's presence and favor into the friendship.

For those of us who are married, studies show that less than 1 percent of couples who pray together will ever get divorced. Less than 1 percent! That's amazing, especially when the divorce rate is over 50 percent in our nation. If you *pray* together there's a 99 percent chance you will *stay* together. The one thing you can do to practically divorce-proof your marriage is pray together, yet many couples rarely do. The reason is that it can be awkward to get started. When I've encouraged couples to pray together, they tell me they don't know how to start—what to pray about. It just seems awkward. But many things are awkward when you first start them. When you started riding a bike, I'm sure it was awkward. When I started playing golf—very awkward. The hardest part is just getting started.

Most of us brush our teeth at least twice a day. In fact, if you're anything like me, you brush your teeth while you're doing one or two other things. You don't even give it a thought. It's something you do automatically. But when a small child is learning to brush their teeth, it's very unnatural at first. They must be instructed how to hold the toothbrush, how much toothpaste to use, not to swallow the toothpaste. But after time, it becomes second nature. So it is with prayer. At first you might feel uncomfortable bringing it up—asking the other person if they will pray with you—but ask anyway.

I mentioned that my father was our premarriage counselor, and he told us that whenever we got into an argument we needed to stop, get into each other's arms, and pray. I remember one of our early arguments when Julie interrupted me and said, "Remember your dad said we're supposed to pray together." I recall thinking, "I don't want to pray with you, woman. Go pray by yourself." Eventually we got into each other's arms and prayed. I wanted to pray, "Lord, help Julie know just how wrong she is," but I refrained. Even though my prayer was not very eloquent or very long, taking the time to stop arguing and ask the Holy Spirit to invade our little home changed everything.

The best defense is a great offense. When you pray *with* each other and *for* each other there are hurtful words that will never be spoken. Fights that will never break out. Apologies that will never have to be given. But the hardest time to start praying is when you're in an argument. In fact, it will be the last thing you want to do. So pray now. Begin to make praying together a part of your everyday life. Normalize it, and when you do, prayer will render doubt powerless in the relationship.

FIGHT *FOR* THE RELATIONSHIP

Usually when conflict happens, we are fighting *against* the other person. Fighting for our voice to be heard. Fighting for what we think is right. We see them as the enemy, but they're not.

"For we are not fighting against flesh-and-blood enemies, but against evil rulers and authorities of the unseen world, against mighty powers in this dark world, and against evil spirits in the heavenly places" (Eph. 6:12). Paul lets us in on a huge secret. We have an enemy, but it's not

> **The best defense is a great offense.**

that person that just set you off. Jesus said, "The thief comes only to steal and kill and destroy" (John 10:10, NIV). Your spiritual enemy wants to destroy your relationship, ruin your marriage, and rob you of your peace. You are in a war zone; just make sure you're not fighting your allies. It's OK to get angry, just make sure you focus that anger at the devil.

When you're in an argument with a friend or your spouse, it's not them, and it's not *about* whatever you're fighting about. It's a spiritual attack on your home, on your relationship, on your joy. It's a frontal attack from your enemy to bring division and stir up doubt and suspicion in the relationship. When you can identify the enemy for who he is, you are able to take him out before he takes the friendship out.

MAKE THE FIRST MOVE

So are you a peacemaker or a peace faker? Are you hoping peace will happen, or are you making it happen, working to resolve the conflict, having the courageous conversations? Are you fighting for peace or just fighting? You have the chance to turn it all around. If you get better, your relationships are guaranteed to get at least 50 percent better because you are 50 percent of every relationship you have.

Who do you need to go to this week? What relationships need to be reconciled? Remember, children reflect the nature of their father, and your heavenly Father is the ultimate Peacemaker. Go be like Him.

WORK OUT THE DOUBT

1. Are you naturally a fighter or a fleer? How does this display itself in your life when conflict happens in a relationship?

2. Conflict won't destroy the relationship, but unresolved conflict will. What relationship in your life has unresolved conflict? What can you do about it?

3. What is the difference between resolution and reconciliation?

Chapter 14

MIND THE GAP

Holding a grudge doesn't make you strong; it makes you bitter. Forgiving doesn't make you weak; it sets you free.
—DAVE WILLIS

WHEN JULIE AND I were first married, I thought it would be great to surprise her with a backpacking trip across Europe. So I purchased two nonrefundable airplane tickets, two Eurail passes, and two backpacks, without ever talking to her about it. I'm a "seven" on the Enneagram, so you could say adventure is my love language. Of course, today I would counsel newlyweds to talk to the other person before making such a purchase, but at twenty-two years old I didn't know any better.

Our first stop was London. On the train from Heathrow airport into the city, we kept hearing words over the speaker system that we couldn't quite make out. They were spoken in a thick British accent, "Mind the gap." Every time the doors opened the voice would repeat the phrase, "Mind the gap." We had no idea what they were saying or what it meant until it was our time to get off the train. As we stepped out of the train, we realized there was an eight- to ten-inch gap between the train and the platform, large enough that you could lose a small child or twist an ankle. Mind the gap. They were telling us to pay attention to the gap.

In our relationships we need to *mind the gap*. When conflict and misunderstanding happen, it creates a gap. A gap between our expectations and our experience. A gap between what we think the other person should have done and what they actually did. When this happens, doubt is the first thing to jump into the gap. Doubt works with our imagination to come up with all sorts of reasons why they did what they did or said what they said. Doubt reminds us of all the times we've been hurt this way before. We have to mind the gap.

Often when the gap first occurs in a relationship, no lasting harm is done. It might be a misunderstanding between friends or a careless word spoken. Regardless, it creates the gap—and what we put in that gap matters. Many times we put silence in the gap. One or both parties shut down and refuse to communicate. The gap widens. If we do talk about the problem, we end up talking to other people. We tell our friends about what that person did or how they made us feel. Now we've put other people in the gap, drawing them into the conflict. Before long the gap has widened, and we begin questioning the other person's motives and commitment.

OVERLOOK THE SMALL THINGS

There are two lessons I've learned that help close the gap quickly. First, we need to overlook the small things. Proverbs 19:11 (GW) says, "A person with good sense is patient, and it is to his credit that he overlooks an offense." Sometimes the littlest things become the biggest problems.

Someone says something that offends us or posts something on social media that we disagree with. It's a small thing that we allow to become a big problem.

It might be when your spouse comes home at the end of a day and they're a little short-tempered. We take it personally when maybe we need to give them a little space. Show a little grace. Or maybe someone at the office looks at you with a scowl on their face. Maybe it's not you at all but the Mexican food they ate at lunch. Let's love people enough to overlook the small things.

A disclaimer here: That doesn't mean we overlook a destructive pattern. It's one thing to come home from work a little short-tempered, but if that's happening every day, you need to address it. There may be an anger issue that needs to be resolved. So if it's a destructive pattern, it's time to talk. Or if their actions are damaging the

> **Sometimes the littlest things become the biggest problems.**

relationship, it's time to have a courageous conversation. In fact, the most loving thing you can do would be to address the issue. And when the gap has widened, making it too difficult for either party to come to the other, it may be time to ask an expert to intervene—like a professional counselor or pastor.

When it's a minor issue we overlook, but when it's a more serious issue we "over-love." To over-love simply means to give more love than required. When you think about a sink that overflows, it has more water than it can hold. When we overeat, we eat more than we need to survive, and we become overweight. All of that means "having more than what is needed." To over-love someone means to give more love in the relationship than what is expected. To be generous with our love. Generous with our kindness, with our words, with our forgiveness.

First Peter 4:8 (AMP) says, "Above all things have intense and unfailing love for one another, for love covers a multitude of sins [forgives and disregards the offenses of others]." The word *intense* in the original language means "straining as a runner strains to win a race." He gives his all. I mentioned earlier that the 2024 Summer Olympics were being held in Paris as I wrote this book. Every night Julie and I tuned in to cheer on Team USA. Our favorite events were track and field. In every race the athletes were "straining to win the race," giving everything they had to cross the finish line. Nothing held back. They left it all on the field.

That's the way we're to love the people in our lives. We must over-love—give more love and grace than what is required. It's the only way we win at our relationships. But this is where doubt comes in. Often the reason we won't overlook or can't over-love is because we've allowed doubt a seat at the table. We doubt the other person's motives. We question why they would treat us this way. We replay all the times they made us feel belittled or criticized. We allow trust to be eroded, oftentimes without ever discussing the problem with the other person.

I have had some amazing conversations—all by myself. I concocted a whole scenario of why that person was treating me the way they did. I planned out all the things I wanted to say to them, but I never got around to the conversation. I was peace faking, not peacemaking.

I remember one time when I did have a courageous conversation with a coworker about how his email was harsh and demeaning. I went to his office and told him how his words had impacted me. He looked at me with a blank stare. He had no idea what I was talking about. So I pulled out my phone and read his email out loud with special emphasis on the words I had found so offensive. When I finished with my dramatic reading, he simply looked up and said, "That's not at all what I meant." Then he proceeded to read the email the way he intended for it to be received. It was a totally different message! I had completely misinterpreted what he was trying to communicate.

I had been walking around for a week frustrated, hurt, and offended. I had chosen to let offense take root in the relationship rather than overlooking the email as a small thing or choosing to over-love my coworker—and at least go have a conversation. Once I did, it exposed how quickly offense can creep in and how doubt can begin to dismantle the friendship.

BELIEVE THE BEST

The second lesson I've learned to close the gap quickly is to believe the best—of both people and situations. In our fast-paced, over-caffeinated lives, it's easy to fall into the trap of assuming the worst, jumping to conclusions, and allowing doubt to cloud our judgment of other people's intentions. As followers of Jesus, we are called to a higher standard. He tells us in Matthew 7:12 (NIV) to "do to others what you would have them do to you." This timeless teaching reminds us to treat others with the same grace, kindness, and understanding that we desire.

Paul reminds us that true love is something that "always protects, always trusts, always hopes, always perseveres" (1 Cor. 13:7, NIV). This kind of love doesn't jump to conclusions; it doesn't assume the worst in someone. Instead, it chooses to see the best in others, to trust their intentions, and to hope for good in every situation. When we love others this way, it builds a foundation for the relationship that is strong and able to stand against the storms. Research has proven that when we assume the best in others it will lead to healthier relationships and personal well-being. People who believe their friend's or partner's intentions are good, even during times of conflict, experience greater satisfaction and stability in their relationship.[1]

In a world that often encourages skepticism and distrust, choosing to believe the best in others is a countercultural act of faith. It's a decision to trust in the goodness that God has placed within each person and remember that everyone is on a journey. In his book *Life Together*, Dietrich Bonhoeffer reminds us that our Christian community is built on a foundation of love and grace. "Judging others makes us blind, whereas love is illuminating. By judging others, we blind ourselves to our own evil and to the grace which others are just as entitled to as we are."[2]

EXTRA GRACE REQUIRED

Sometimes you can't overlook or just over-love. Sometimes extra grace is required, an unnatural grace. Forgiveness is a vital component to every relationship. Every lasting friendship is made up of two great forgivers. Colossians 3:13 (NIV) says, "Bear with each other and forgive one another.... Forgive as the Lord forgave you." Think about the way God has forgiven you. Completely. Without hesitation or reservation. Psalm 86 (NKJV) says the Lord is "ready to forgive." James 5:11 (NIV) tells us "the Lord is full of compassion and mercy." He's not stingy with His forgiveness. He gives it freely. That's the way we're supposed to forgive others.

Our human nature is to not forgive—or at least not be *quick* to forgive. We want the other person to pay for what they've done. We tend to hold on to the hurt. Carry the grudge. We're afraid forgiveness somehow excuses the other person's behavior. If we forgive them, it's as if what they did was no big deal. But actually having to forgive the person acknowledges that what they did *was* a big deal—so big that it requires forgiveness.

A few lessons I have learned about forgiveness when it comes to my relationships:

Forgiveness is not a feeling, it's a choice. If you wait until you feel like it—you won't. Forgiveness is an act of the will. You *get* to choose to love the other person, to forgive the way Jesus has forgiven you and ultimately release yourself from carrying it around. You're making the choice to allow the Holy Spirit to empower you to do something you could never do on your own: forgive someone for what they have done to you.

Forgiveness is not forgetting. The scar of what the other person said or did may never leave your memory. Once you forgive that person, you're not going to have memory loss and instantly forget what happened. Only God is able to throw our sins as far as the east is from the west (Ps. 103:12) and remember our sin no more (Heb. 8:12). You're not Him. Forgiveness is a onetime acknowledgment; healing is a process.

Forgiveness is not the same as trust. Forgiveness can be given instantly. Trust takes time. (We will talk more about trust in the next chapter.) Just because you forgive someone for what they did doesn't mean you can immediately trust them. Transparency, plus consistency, plus time will build back trust in the relationship.

Two Sides, Same Coin

When it comes to forgiveness, there is both *giving* forgiveness and *seeking* forgiveness. And for any relationship to be great you must get great at both. Seeking forgiveness is being responsible for my part of the problem. I might be 98 percent right and 2 percent wrong, but I need to

> **Forgiveness is a onetime acknowledgment; healing is a process.**

take 100 percent responsibility for my 2 percent.

Seeking forgiveness means apologizing correctly. Have you ever heard a bad apology? "I'm sorry you were so easily offended by what I said." "I'm sorry you took it the wrong way." "I'm sorry, but if you had just done what I told you to do, this never would have happened." All bad apologies. (I actually might have said one or two of those before.)

There are four steps you must take when asking someone for forgiveness:

1. **Admit you were wrong**. Be specific. Own up to it. No "ifs" or "buts" allowed. Own 100 percent of your part.

2. **Accept the consequences**. Even if the other person forgives you, there may be consequences to your actions. Don't try to avoid taking responsibility. Accept the consequences.

3. **Alter your behavior.** Don't say you're sorry and then go right back and continue doing what you did. Let your actions prove that you're truly sorry.

4. **Allow time.** Sometimes the offense goes so deep that it takes time to heal. Allow the time. Don't expect everything to go back to the way it was after one apology. "I said I was sorry. Why can't we just move on?" Allow time to build back trust.

SOMETIMES FORGIVENESS IS NOT ENOUGH

There are times when you will forgive the other person and they will forgive you, but the relationship still remains fractured. I've had situations where I sought forgiveness and gave forgiveness, and still the relationship was broken. Peace and unity are high values in my life to the extent that I've gone the third and fourth mile trying to build a bridge back to the other person, only to find they did not want to cross it. As hard as I tried, they were not in a place to be able to restore the friendship. Romans 12:18 (NIV) has helped me in moments like these: "As far as it depends on you, live at peace with everyone."

As far as it depends on you. Some things *don't* depend on you. You can't control the other person or their readiness to restore the relationship. You can't control their response; you are only responsible for you. Seek forgiveness humbly. Give forgiveness freely. Do the hard work at closing the gap, and then allow the Holy Spirit to do the work that only He can do.

WORK OUT THE DOUBT

1. Colossians 3:13 (NIV) says, "Bear with each other and forgive one another....Forgive as the Lord forgave you." Write out how the Lord forgave you. How does this verse challenge you regarding forgiveness?

2. Take a moment to reflect on what forgiveness is and what it is not. Ask God to show you if there is someone you need to forgive. Write down what you need to forgive them for.

3. Ask the Lord if there is someone you need to apologize to. Take time today to write a note seeking their forgiveness.

Chapter 15

TRUST: BUILDING BACK WHAT'S BROKEN

*Trust takes years to build, seconds to
break, and a lifetime to repair.*
—UNKNOWN

I WAS YOUNG AND just starting out in ministry. The
church had moved into our first permanent facility,
and we were experiencing tremendous growth. More
people were coming to faith and joining the church than
we ever imagined. One of my jobs was to gather and train
volunteers to make follow-up calls to all the visitors. Some
weeks we would each have twenty or more phone calls to
make. If people didn't get followed up with, they wouldn't
feel cared for and they might not come back.

One of my many downfalls is that I have a high sense
of urgency. And while that helps me get things done, it
can also come off as demanding. At the young age of
twenty-four, I hadn't had the latter revelation yet. I'm sure
my urgency came across as annoying and critical at times.
(My sincere apologies to all the people I was leading in my
twenties. Thank you for bearing with me.)

During this season, one of my volunteers asked to meet
with me. He came to my office, sat down, and seemed
upset. Something I had said in a meeting got back to him,

and he wanted to talk about it. He confronted me with what he had heard, and immediately I remembered the words coming out of my mouth. Earlier that week I had been in a meeting trying to solve a problem, and in the heat of the moment I said something that put my friend in a negative light. When he confronted me, I instantly felt ashamed. I admitted I said it, but I tried to explain the context. It was too late. The damage was done. Trust had been broken. My friend went on to say he forgave me, but this made him question my integrity in leadership. His words stung, but he was right.

I was devastated. I never meant to hurt my friend. I never should have said what I said in that meeting. I was completely responsible for trust being broken. The next several months were strained between us. Me trying to be overly nice. Him, very reserved. Over time our relationship healed. We never got back to the place we were before, but close. Surprisingly, I look back on that event with gratitude. I'm grateful it happened early in my leadership journey. It taught me a lot about the power of trust and the impact it has when it's broken.

FIRM FOUNDATION

Trust is the foundation of any meaningful relationship. Whether it's between friends, spouses, or business partners, trust serves as the glue that holds the relationship together. It includes elements of reliability, integrity, and vulnerability. It is the confidence we place in someone to act in our best interest, to be honest, and to honor their commitments. In Stephen Covey's book *The Speed of Trust*, he states, "Trust is the one thing that changes everything."[1] It accelerates relationships, deepens connections, and fosters a sense of security.

You cannot have a vibrant relationship without trust. Your marriage needs it. Your kids need it. Your coworkers need it. Trust will give your relationships strength, fortitude, and resilience. It creates a sense of security that allows people to be vulnerable, to open up, to share their true feelings without fear of being judged or rejected or hurt. This type of vulnerability is critical to developing a meaningful connection.

Over the past several years Julie and I have worked to build this kind of trust with our Lead Team, the six people that help us lead the church. Don't get me wrong; we've always had incredible trust for the people we work with, and they trust us, but we realized we had not been intentional about building trust. We had put trust on "cruise control."

We started by taking the team through Covey's book *The Speed of Trust* (a must read). We identified where trust on our team was strong and where it was not. We called out the behaviors that build trust and those that tear it down. We identified the places in our past where trust had been weakened and the impact low trust had on our team. It was a tedious process.

Up to this point, we assumed everyone knew how to build trust and how to avoid the actions and attitudes that could erode it. We had hoped that trust would grow on its own, but trust needs to be cultivated. We must feed the behaviors that grow trust and weed out the ones that poison it.

As a team we identified our new "rules of engagement"— the way we would interact with each other. We clarified expectations and normalized accountability. We positioned accountability as a friend, there to help you keep the commitments you made. Our team tended not to ask each other for help, either because we knew everyone was busy or we didn't want to appear as incompetent. We identified that as a trustbuster and celebrated when someone on the team asked for help. We recognized that our collective talent and ability is greater than any one of us alone.

All of this began to cultivate trust. We found ourselves communicating more with each other. Walls came down and relationships grew stronger. As a result, we enjoyed working together more. Our relationship connection increased as trust increased. As a team and as individuals we were more fulfilled in our jobs as trust grew in our relationships.

> **Trust will give your relationships strength, fortitude, and resilience.**

Research has found that higher levels of trust lead to more effective communication and greater relationship satisfaction. This study stated that trust reduces the fear of being misunderstood or rejected, allowing for more honest and constructive conversations. As a result, team members feel comfortable taking risks and exploring opportunities that bring the organization success.[2]

FAMILY VALUES

Trust isn't just needed in the work environment. Trust needs to be built stronger in every relationship you have. You can have a conversation with your spouse or family or a friend and identify the words or actions that foster trust in the relationship and the ones that tear it down. You can take time as a family to write out your rules of engagement—what is acceptable and what is not. As you listen to the people in your life, you'll begin to understand how you can build trust in the relationships and strengthen the emotional bonds you have with them.

In his book *The Four Loves*, C. S. Lewis highlights the importance of trust in fostering deep emotional connections. He writes,

> To love at all is to be vulnerable. Love anything, and your heart will certainly be wrung and possibly be broken. If you want to make sure of keeping it intact, you must give your heart to no one, not even to an animal. Wrap it carefully round with hobbies and little luxuries; avoid all entanglements; lock it up safe in the casket or coffin of your selfishness. But in that casket—safe, dark, motionless, airless— it will change. It will not be broken; it will become unbreakable, impenetrable, irredeemable.[3]

Lewis' words are both sobering and true. He warns the reader that trust is necessary for love to flourish. Without trust, walls stay high. We lose our connection with others and lock ourselves away from the intimacy we've been created for. But what do we do when trust is broken? How fragile is it, and can it be rebuilt once shattered?

The Fragility of Trust

The problem with trust is that it is inherently fragile. It takes years to build but can be shattered in an instant. The fragility lies in its foundation of expectations and consistency. When these expectations are broken, the impact can be devastating. We begin to doubt that we can ever trust that person again. Doubt and insecurity seep into the foundation of the relationship, causing walls to go up.

Covey describes distrust as expensive. When trust is broken, the emotional and relational costs are high. Miscommunications, suspicion, and insecurity work their way into the relationship, causing further damage. Communication breaks down, mutual respect diminishes, and the emotional bond weakens.

We've all been in a friendship or relationship where trust was broken. Something was said or done that couldn't be overlooked or over-loved. It was deeper than that. It was betrayal. And when that betrayal comes from a spouse or close friend or

> The problem with trust is that it is inherently fragile.

business partner, it can cause you to wonder if the relationship can be repaired. Can you ever trust again?

When trust is broken there are two distinct pathways forward, one for the person who was betrayed and the other for the betrayer. The lion's share of work to rebuild trust lies on the one who broke it in the first place. Theirs is the job of rebuilding, and this building project takes time.

BECOMING TRUSTWORTHY

Rebuilding trust, although challenging, is possible. It requires intentional effort, patience, and a genuine commitment to change. Whether it's a personal or professional relationship, it is a delicate and gradual process. It can't happen overnight and requires a series of consistent, trustworthy actions over time.

Simply put, to build trust you have to be trustworthy. That word breaks down as "worthy of trust." The way you become worthy of trust is by daily, consistent actions that reestablish your credibility and dependability. You *do* what you say you're going to do. You *are* who you say you are. Nothing hidden. Full transparency.

This is more than making promises. It requires taking clear steps to alter your behavior. Covey emphasizes the importance of behavior in rebuilding trust. "You can't talk yourself out of a problem you behaved yourself into. You have to behave yourself out of it."[4] Your changed behavior is the proof that you're committed to rebuilding the relationship.

True repentance is more than an apology. It's about changing your actions. It involves understanding how your behavior impacted the other person, and your remorse motivates you to do whatever you must to rebuild trust. The word *repent* means to change direction. It's as if you were heading in one direction and you stop, do a 180-degree turn, and head in the opposite direction. It's a clear change.

> Simply put, to build trust you have to be trustworthy.

But the key ingredient to becoming trustworthy is consistency. It takes time. Don't expect the other person to "forgive and forget." Only God can do that, but your consistent effort to walk in integrity and character will build trust back into the relationship.

FINDING FORGIVENESS

The hardest part of rebuilding trust is not on the one who broke trust but on the one who was betrayed. They didn't see this coming. They are not remotely responsible for the trust being destroyed, but they have a critical role in it being rebuilt.

When you've been hurt by someone close, it can be hard to forgive. If the wound is still fresh, you may not want to forgive. Maybe you think you don't have the strength to forgive. We've already mentioned that forgiveness is not forgetting or saying the offense was not a big deal. Forgiveness is a choice. And you are the only one who can make it.

When I find myself not wanting to forgive someone who has hurt me, or perhaps I don't think I have enough grace to extend to them, I pray this prayer: "God, I don't want to forgive them. I don't think they deserve my forgiveness. But I know that I don't deserve the forgiveness You've shown to me. You have loved me and forgiven me time and time again. So I pray that the grace You've shown to me would flow through me toward them."

In his book *The Weight of Glory*, C. S. Lewis writes, "To be a Christian means to forgive the inexcusable because God has forgiven the inexcusable in you."[5] When you believe you don't have the capacity to love and forgive the other person, don't rely on your own capacity. Tap into the grace God has shown you. Lean into the love He has poured over your life and extend that same grace and love to the person who's offended you.

Stronger Than Ever

While trust is fragile, it is not beyond repair. Years ago I learned about the Japanese art of kintsugi. Kintsugi literally translates as "golden repair." It is the practice of mending broken pottery or glass with gold or other fine metals. The gold becomes the glue that holds the broken pieces together. The gold binding creates a bond that makes the pottery more resistant to future breaks. It's literally stronger than it was before. And because of the gold now integrated into the bowl or vase, the piece is more valuable than it was before it was broken.[6]

That's a picture of what can happen when trust is rebuilt in a relationship. The repair is tedious and takes time, but because of the authenticity and vulnerability used in the repair, it comes back stronger than before. Because of the investment and dedication of both the one building trust and the one giving it, there is an increased sense of value to the relationship.

Trust is the most valuable gift you can give to any relationship. If it's missing, you can work to repair it. It's a tedious work, but the rewards are priceless.

WORK OUT THE DOUBT

1. Think about a relationship where trust has been broken. What can you do to begin to rebuild it?

2. What do you need to do to become a person who is worthy of trust?

3. What is the difference between apologizing and rebuilding trust?

Chapter 16

WHEN DOUBT DEVELOPS
YOUR CHARACTER

Every problem is a character-building opportunity.
—RICK WARREN

J UNE 5, 2020, was a day I will cherish forever. It was a day filled with promise and new beginnings. A day forged in prayer. It was the day that Jefferson and Cassie got married! Julie and I were sitting at the reception, fighting back tears as we watched the bride and groom dance. All around the room were so many of the people who had been with us on this journey, family and dear friends who had carried us in prayer and literally prayed this day into existence.

I remember sitting there thinking, "It doesn't get any better than this. This is what life is all about." Our kids were happy and in love. Our family and friends were there celebrating with us. People who had walked with us every step of the way were there to witness this remarkable step. It just doesn't get any better than this.

Maybe you've made a similar statement at a remarkable moment in your life. The birth of a child. Sitting around a campfire with good friends. A moment where all the world seemed right and you thought to yourself, "It doesn't get any better than this." If you have, I can guarantee that there were other people involved. That moment held such value because of the people who made it happen. Good chance you didn't utter those words sitting alone eating ice cream, watching Netflix. Those are good moments; they're just not the best moments of life. The best moments always include other people.

There may be other times when you've thought, "It doesn't get any *worse* than this." Something happened, and you feel like your world is falling apart. You're not sure if you're ever going to recover from what you experienced. Again, there's high probability your pain is a result of people. Someone hurt you. Let you down. Broke your trust. And you're sitting in your disappointment and disbelief wondering if you can move forward.

The Best of Times and the Worst of Times Both Involve People

Sometimes people give you a great reason to doubt them. They break your trust. They go back on their promise. They prove to be untrustworthy. In moments like these, doubt is the reasonable response. Taking time to question if that person is worthy of your trust can help protect you from prolonged pain. Even when you have every reason to doubt, you can make sure it doesn't take you out. You can learn to leverage life's hardest moments to make you better.

There's a guy in the Bible who experienced the *best of times* and the *worst of times* all at the hands of other people. People he should have been able to trust proved to be completely untrustworthy.

In the tapestry of Genesis, one of the most compelling

stories is that of Joseph. His journey is a picture of overcoming betrayal, maintaining faith, and refusing to let doubt disrupt his connection with others. Favored by his father, Joseph was a target for his brothers' jealousy. After sharing his dreams that would one day put him in a place of authority over them, they attacked Joseph, threw him in a pit, and sold him into slavery in Egypt.

Joseph ends up serving in the house of Potiphar, one of Pharaoh's officers. Scripture doesn't tell us what happened in those early days, but we do know Joseph didn't allow his disappointment to get the best of him. He obviously worked hard and proved himself, because soon Potiphar puts him in charge of his entire household. That type of promotion doesn't happen if you're sitting around complaining about what has happened to you. It happens when you don't allow doubt and disappointment to take you out of the game.

> You can learn to leverage life's hardest moments to make you better.

Potiphar's wife (one of the first cougars in the Bible) notices how handsome young Joseph is and tries to seduce him. But Joseph doesn't compromise his integrity. He doesn't buy into the advertisement that what happens in Egypt stays in Egypt, and he runs away from the temptress, only to be falsely accused and thrown in prison.

Once again we don't read about Joseph pleading his case to the warden or asking for a retrial. He simply goes to work where he finds himself. He remains faithful. And once again Joseph is put in charge. The warden entrusts the running of his prison to an inmate.

If you're familiar with the rest of the story, Joseph interprets the dreams of two other prisoners, Pharaoh's baker and cupbearer. Both of his interpretations come true, and the baker is executed while the cupbearer returns to the palace. Joseph's only request: "Don't forget about me." Which is exactly what the cupbearer does, for two more years, until Pharaoh has a dream that no one can interpret. When the cupbearer remembers a man in prison who could interpret dreams, Joseph is brought before Pharaoh to interpret his dream.

Pharaoh's dream is a revelation of a coming famine in the region. Jospeh interprets the dream and advises Pharaoh that the seven years of plenty will prepare his kingdom for the seven years of drought. Overwhelmed by Joseph's wisdom, Pharaoh puts him in charge of his entire kingdom, second only to Pharaoh himself.

Joseph goes from the best of times as his father's favored child, to the worst of times with his brothers selling him into slavery, to the best of times overseeing Potiphar's house, to the worst of times being falsely accused and thrown in prison, to being put in charge of the prison, to being forgotten, to becoming second-in-command of Pharaoh's kingdom. Talk about emotional whiplash.

All along the way, Joseph had every reason not to trust people. He had been hurt so many times it would have been easy for him to grow bitter and angry. He could have justified giving up. Throwing in the towel. Building up walls to keep others out. But Jospeh didn't let his doubt and disappointment debilitate him. He didn't become paralyzed by his pain.

Often, when we are hurt by people, we become angry and disenchanted. We allow the pain we've experienced to paralyze us, keeping us from moving forward. Joseph's story teaches us: People pain is inevitable, but it doesn't have to be terminal.

People Pain Is Inevitable, But It Doesn't Have to Be Terminal

When I get hurt by people, I tend to shut down. Go inward. Focus on the pain of what happened and how it made me feel. Every time I respond that way, I lose. Game over. I remain paralyzed in whatever place the other person's actions have put me. But when I remember to do what Joseph did, I can turn the pain into a payoff.

When we look at the ups and downs of Joseph's life, there's one thing that remained consistent: *his posture.* Joseph kept an open posture toward God. Life open. Arms open. Regardless of the circumstances. And as a result, God stayed open to working in Joseph's life and situations, even the ones he didn't choose for himself. Many times we forget that God can work in any and every situation, and He specializes in the impossible ones. Often the only limitation is our posture: Are we looking up to God, crying out for His help, or are we consumed with the problem and angry with the people that got us there?

Think about David. He faced many unfavorable situations in his life, but his posture of dependence on God opened the door for God to move in power through his life. Or Gideon; his posture of obedience positioned him to be used by God to defeat the Midianites and set his people free. Or in the case of Joseph, whether he was in a pit or serving Potiphar or cleaning the prison, his posture of trusting God opened the door for God to move in his life.

In fact, we see God using the doubt and disappointment to develop Joseph's character and help him become the man he dreamed he could be. Without his journey from the pit to the prison, Joseph wouldn't have been ready for the palace. It was the pit and the prison that prepared him for his assignment.

As Jacob's favored child, it's safe to assume he was given special treatment. We know his father gave him an ornate robe to wear. Scholars believe this "coat of many colors" would have resembled a wedding garment in that day. Good chance he wasn't cleaning the barns or doing manual labor in a wedding gown.

> **Many times we forget that God can work in any and every situation, and He specializes in the impossible ones.**

But his journey to Egypt and the suffering he endured developed a spirit of determination and perseverance in young Joseph. He would find his strength in God to not give up. It would be thirteen years from the pit to the palace. Thirteen years of delays and disappointments before the dreams would be fulfilled.

When Joseph was young and brash, he bragged to his brothers about his dreams, that one day he would rule over them. He wasn't sinful; he just wasn't wise. But the years of navigating difficult people and complicated situations taught him wisdom, to the point that Pharaoh commended Joseph for his wisdom, saying, "There is none so discerning and wise" as Jospeh. But Joseph didn't possess that wisdom before the pit.

Every step of his journey was developing his character.

Every delay was forging his dependence on God. From his time in the pit when his future was unknown, to the years serving in Potiphar's house, to being falsely accused and thrown in prison, every day he had to learn to trust God. Dependency was forged through the disappointment.

But probably the greatest character development in Joseph's life came after his promotion. After the seven years of plenty. After the years of success. Just about the time he thought he had learned all the lessons God needed to teach him, he was about to learn his most difficult one yet. It occurred when his brothers traveled to Egypt because the famine had spread to Canaan. To receive the grain they needed, they found themselves bowing before the governor of the land, Joseph. They didn't recognize him, but Joseph recognized them. And in the following chapters as Joseph deals with his brothers, God is dealing with Joseph, teaching him the most important lesson of all: grace.

Joseph could have retaliated. He had every right to lash out and get even with his brothers for the pain they caused, but God wanted to instruct Joseph in the grace of forgiveness. A quality so integrated into the character and nature of God that He would give His only Son to sinners so that we could understand how extraordinary grace truly is.

A LESSON WE ALL MUST LEARN

Grace is the one lesson God requires that we all learn, and the only way we can learn it is by being betrayed, let down, disappointed. Learning to forgive others requires that others break your trust. That they do something so egregious that it requires grace—so momentous that it requires mercy. Forgiveness is a critical lesson in our character development because grace and mercy define our relationship with God. God is a really good forgiver, and He wants His children to become like Him.

"God demonstrates his own love for us in this: While we were still sinners, Christ died for us" (Rom. 5:8, NIV). God didn't wait for us to recognize our need for His forgiveness before He sent His Son. That's how committed to forgiveness He is. The reason forgiveness is so important to God is because *relationship* is so important to God, and you can't experience relationship without forgiveness.

> God is a really good forgiver, and He wants His children to become like Him.

God wants you to become really good at forgiving others, but the only way you can become good at something is to repeat it often. And to repeat forgiveness means there will be people in your life that you have to forgive over and over again.

PRACTICE MAKES PERFECT

Athletes master a skill by repeated practice. The athletes that compete in the Olympics will prepare four years for their event. They will practice nearly every day for 1,460 days before the next Olympic Games take place. Swimmers will swim 80,000 meters a week in training, which converts to 1,600 laps in a pool. That's more than 333,000 laps in four years. That's a lot of practice for a swimming competition.

And while the Olympic Games are amazing and really

important, they are not as important as your relationships. God wants you to win at what matters most, so He will put you in the pool with other people to swim laps. He'll sign you up for a 4 x 400-meter relay race so you have to learn to swim together with others. Teammates will let you down, so you'll have ample opportunity to learn how to show grace and forgiveness. And God will keep you in the pool, swimming laps, until you become proficient in grace.

Winning at What Matters Most

Perseverance. Integrity. Patience. Grace. They are all a part of your character development regimen, and God cares more about your character than anything you can ever accomplish. He will go to great lengths to refine your character, because in the end it's your character that carries eternal significance. Talents and abilities are gifts from God, no doubt about it. They're the tools He gives us to fulfill His purposes in our lives. But without the foundation of a godly character, even the most remarkable talent can become a stumbling block.

Proverbs 22:1 (NIV) reminds us, "A good name is more desirable than great riches; to be esteemed is better than silver or gold." A "good name" refers to one's reputation, which is rooted in character. God values who you *are* more than what you *do*.

Think about King David. He was anointed as a young shepherd, and he developed a great talent as a warrior and leader. Yet it wasn't his talent that qualified him to be king—it was his heart. In 1 Samuel 16:7 (NIV), God says to Samuel, "The LORD does not look at the things people look at. People look at the outward appearance, but the LORD looks at the heart." David's character, shaped by his time in the fields with God, was what made him a man after God's own heart. It wasn't his ability to defeat Goliath or lead an army; it was his humility, his integrity, and his faith in God, even when others let him down.

THE REFINING PROCESS

The truth is, God is more interested in refining your character than in showcasing your talents. I've found the refining process is uncomfortable, but completely necessary for our growth. James 1:2–4 tells us, "Consider it pure joy, my brothers and sisters, whenever you face trials of many kinds, because you know that the testing of your faith produces perseverance. Let perseverance finish its work so that you may be mature and complete, not lacking anything." Challenges and disappointments in life, often because people let us down, are what God uses to build us up and shape us into the person He wants us to be.

I believe God allows difficulties in our lives not to break us but to refine us. Just as gold is refined by fire, God wants to refine our character through the fires of life's challenges. When we go through tough times, our true character is revealed. It's in those moments that God works on our heart, purging away impurities like pride, selfishness, and fear. Our sufferings aren't meaningless; they produce something of eternal value. It's producing character that will carry us not just through this life but into eternity.

In a world that often values talent over character, we have to remember that God's economy operates differently.

He cares more about who we are *becoming* than what we are *accomplishing*. Our character is the only thing we will take with us into eternity, and it's the one thing that God is continually working to refine.

So stay in the pool. Practice your laps. Become skilled at the grace of forgiveness, and let doubt and disappointment develop your character, causing you to win at what matters most.

WORK OUT THE DOUBT

1. "People pain" is inevitable, but it doesn't have to be terminal. When was a time you allowed the pain inflicted by another person to paralyze you?

2. Looking back, how do you wish you had responded?

3. How has God used disappointment in a relationship to develop your character?

Conclusion

HELPING OTHERS KICK OUT DOUBT

When fear knocks at your door, send faith to answer it.
—Unknown

Y our journey with doubt isn't a short sprint or a onetime altercation. It's more like a marathon or an endless boxing match with a persistent opponent that keeps trying to take you down. My self-doubt started in elementary school, but it didn't end there. Recently I was battling insecurity and feeling down on myself. I was listening to the lies banging around in my head. At just the right time Julie walked into my office, wrapped her arms around me, and told me what a great husband I was. She told me how I was the best dad Jefferson could ever ask for, and that I was a great leader and pastor. She had no idea I was battling doubt at that moment, but *her words* replaced the words I was speaking over myself.

Those times when I still doubt God's goodness or question His promises, it will be the words of a trusted friend that reminds me of God's faithfulness and points out all the answered prayers I've experienced. And when I find myself hurt by what someone said or did, and I get defensive and build up walls, it's a brother in Christ who gives me a different perspective and challenges me to respond biblically and have the courageous conversation.

Sometimes we need help to take out doubt. We need the faith of a friend to remind us of what we know to be true. And in the same way, God wants to use you to help someone who's been knocked down by doubt and disappointment.

Faith of a Friend

There's a remarkable story in the Gospel of Mark when Jesus goes back to Capernaum, a small town on the shore of the Sea of Galilee. The news of this miracle-working rabbi had spread throughout the region, and a large crowd had gathered in a house to hear Jesus teach. Four men wanted to get their paralyzed friend to Jesus, hoping He could heal him. But as they arrived at the house, the crowd was so large there was no way in. These four visionaries didn't let that stop them. They climbed on the roof, dug a hole in the ceiling, and lowered their crippled friend down to Jesus. Can you imagine being in that house that day and pieces of the roof start falling in? Could you imagine if that were *your* house? You might not be as excited about the rest of the story if you had an unwanted skylight above your bedroom.

After they lowered the man down to Jesus, the text says, "When Jesus saw their faith, he said to the paralyzed man, 'Son, your sins are forgiven....But I want you to know that the Son of Man has authority on earth to forgive sins.' So he said to the man, 'I tell you, get up, take your mat and go home.' He got up, took his mat and walked out in full view of them all. This amazed everyone and they praised God, saying, 'We have never seen anything like this!'" (Mark 2:5, 10–12). There are a few final lessons we can learn from this story as we help others deal with their doubt.

Pick Up the Mat

We don't know the backstory of the paralyzed man and his four friends. We don't know how long this man had been crippled or what put him in this position. All we do know is that his friends were willing to do the heavy lifting. They were willing to carry their friend to Jesus, and when they realized they could not get through the door, their determination carried them up on the roof. Their faith found a way.

> Sometimes we need help to take out doubt. We need the faith of a friend to remind us of what we know to be true.

Helping people is hard work. Helping someone who is emotionally or psychologically paralyzed can seem impossible. As a pastor, I have spent countless hours counseling and coaching people who feel like life has dealt them an unfair blow. They were knocked down one too many times, and they don't think they have the strength to get back up.

I'm sure you know people like that as well. People who have been crippled by life. They've found themselves on an emotional or spiritual stretcher, watching life pass them by. I'm also sure you have tried to encourage them, pray for them. Maybe you've gone out of your way to help them, and it's not been met with much gratitude. They might have even lashed out at you. When that happens, it's easy to justify dropping their mat and moving on with your life. It's fairly obvious they don't want your help. Or do they?

Could it be they've been dropped by well-meaning people before? Friends who said they would be there for them, who never came through on their promises? People who gave up because the mat was too heavy, too cumbersome? The doorway was blocked, and what was required was more than they could give?

I've found that hurting people hurt people. They don't mean to, but their pain and disappointment speak on their behalf. They often lash out from a place of self-preservation. They can't get their hopes up again. But if we allow their pain to push us away, who will carry them to Jesus?

This man on the mat obviously couldn't get to Jesus on his own. He needed someone to help him. And these four friends rearranged their lives. Whatever they planned to do that day changed. This was going to take time. It would require effort. There's nothing easy or convenient about carrying a paralyzed man across town on a blanket, but his friends were ready to do the heavy lifting.

Years ago a woman in our church was going through an incredibly rough season. It seemed like everyone had walked out on her; her husband, her family, even some of her own children didn't want to have much to do with her. Depression set in, and she wanted to give up on life. She ended up alone and emotionally paralyzed.

But then some ladies from our church who had been in her small group years before found out what had happened. They took her in their home and gave her time to heal. They helped her with everything from her legal battles to her laundry. They cleaned her house and created a home that her children could come back to. My wife, Julie, was one of the women in that small group. I saw firsthand what it required from her to carry her friend to Jesus. There was some heavy lifting, times the doorway was blocked and it would have been easier to set the mat down and try another day.

But it was the faith and hard work of friends that carried this woman to the only place she could find true healing: Jesus. Today Julie's friend is healthy and strong, and the relationships with her children are restored. What I know is that she couldn't have gotten there on her own. She needed the faith of a friend.

Push Through the Mess

Helping people can get messy. The four men in this story didn't let the mess deter their mission. When they arrived at the house and saw the crowd blocking the door, they could have said, "Sorry, buddy. We can't make it in. Maybe the next time Jesus is in town we can try again." But they weren't looking for an excuse, they were looking for Jesus.

> If we allow their pain to push us away, who will carry them to Jesus?

So they climbed on the roof and started to dig. It's important to note that the houses and roofs in this day were made of a mixture of mud and manure. So when they were digging through the roof, they were digging through dried manure. Most of the time you have to dig through some "crap" to get someone to Jesus. Excuse my bluntness, but what they're in right now stinks. What they're wading through is deep. We have to be prepared to push through the mess and not allow a little manure to keep us from our mission.

When you jump in to help someone working through their doubts, anxieties, and fears, it's going to get messy. What has left them paralyzed was painful and complicated. Be committed to helping them get back up. Be committed to helping them process their pain and questions. Be a part of rewriting their story.

PREPARE FOR THE UNEXPECTED

The good news is that when we push through the mess and get people to Jesus, He can do more for them than we can dream or imagine. At the end of that story, when the man got up and walked out of the house, it says, "This amazed everyone and they praised God, saying, 'We have never seen anything like this'" (Mark 2:12). Those people had never witnessed a miraculous move of God like this before.

If we're going to see some things we've never seen before, we have to do some things we've never done before. That man wasn't healed because of his faith or his ability to get himself to Jesus. He was healed because of his friends' faith and their willingness to carry him to Jesus.

Remember what it said when Jesus looked up and saw the man being lowered down through the roof: "When Jesus saw their faith, he said to the paralyzed man, 'Son, your sins are forgiven'" (Mark 2:5, NIV). It wasn't the paralyzed man's faith. We don't know if he had any faith. It was the faith of his friends. Their faith brought this man salvation and healing. Which tells me, we can believe for others what they cannot believe for themselves. Our faith can carry them.

There are spiritual things you have seen that others have not seen. Things that you have heard that they have never heard. Your faith is stronger. Your faith can carry them. But you have to pick them up and get them to Jesus.

DON'T LET DOUBT TAKE THEM OUT

The battle with doubt is not yours alone. Many people around you, family and friends and coworkers, are silently struggling with their own doubts, questioning their own self-worth, doubting God's goodness, or dealing with disappointment in others.

God has sovereignly placed you in their lives for a purpose. You have the opportunity and the responsibility to be a source of hope and strength for them. It is often in the simple moments of a conversation, in an act of kindness, that you can make the most profound impact. Be attentive to the needs of those around you, and be willing to step into their lives with the compassion and grace that Christ has shown you. Your role as a believer is not only to stand firm in your own faith but also to help others find theirs.

One of life's greatest joys is helping others find what you've found. That's why when you eat at a new restaurant with amazing food, or watch the latest hit movie, you can't help but talk about it with your friends. You want them to experience what you experienced. So if we do that when we find great food or see an amazing movie, why wouldn't we do that to help them find freedom? Why wouldn't we take the time to pick up their mat and help them find faith? Don't let doubt take them out. (See Appendix E: "Helping a Friend Kick Out Doubt.")

DEFEATING DOUBT

Doubt can be a destructive force. It can lead us to question our own value, to mistrust God's promises, and to become suspicious of those around us. If left unchecked, doubt has the potential to destroy our most vital relationships— our connection with God, our bond with others, and ultimately the purpose God has put on our lives. We must be determined not to let doubt take us out.

> Your role as a believer is not only to stand firm in your own faith but also to help others find theirs.

But this will be a daily battle. Every day you will have to choose faith over doubt, trust over fear, and love over suspicion. Remember that doubt is not simply a feeling to be dismissed; it's a challenge to be confronted with the truth of God's Word. Your identity is in Christ. You are redeemed by His grace. He has not given you a spirit of fear or worry or anxiety but of power and love and a sound mind.

When doubt tries to creep back in, don't let the seeds get planted. Combat it with the Word of God. Speak God's truth over yourself, your circumstances, and your relationships. Seize it as an opportunity to replace the lies with the truth. Don't allow doubt to become a dead end but a doorway to deeper faith, greater courage, and more intimate relationships with the people you love.

WORK OUT THE DOUBT

1. Write the names of two people in your life who need your help defeating doubt. What are one or two ways that you can help them? (See Appendix E for ideas.)

   I can help _____

   and _____

   by _____

   _____

2. Take time this week to help them. Make the phone call. Send the text. Pray for them every day. Your faith can help them kick out their doubt.

WHO I AM IN CHRIST

I Am Accepted

I am God's child.	But to all who believed him and accepted him, he gave the right to become children of God (John 1:12).
I am Christ's friend.	I no longer call you slaves, because a master doesn't confide in his slaves. Now you are my friends, since I have told you everything the Father told me (John 15:15).
I have been made right with God.	Therefore, since we have been made right in God's sight by faith, we have peace with God because of what Jesus Christ our Lord has done for us (Rom. 5:1).
I have been bought with a price.	Don't you realize that your body is the temple of the Holy Spirit, who lives in you and was given to you by God? You do not belong to yourself, for God bought you with a high price. So you must honor God with your body (1 Cor. 6:19–20).
I am a member of Christ's body.	All of you together are Christ's body, and each of you is a part of it (1 Cor. 12:27).
I have been adopted as God's child.	God decided in advance to adopt us into his own family by bringing us to himself through Jesus Christ. This is what he wanted to do, and it gave him great pleasure (Eph. 1:5).
I have direct access to God.	Now all of us can come to the Father through the same Holy Spirit because of what Christ has done for us (Eph. 2:18).

I have been forgiven of all my sins.	His dear Son...purchased our freedom and forgave our sins (Col. 1:13–14).
I am complete in Christ.	So you also are complete through your union with Christ, who is the head over every ruler and authority (Col. 2:10).

I Am Safe

I am free from condemnation.	So now there is no condemnation for those who belong to Christ Jesus. And because you belong to him, the power of the life-giving Spirit has freed you from the power of sin that leads to death (Rom. 8:1–2).
I know God is working for my good.	And we know that God causes everything to work together for the good of those who love God and are called according to his purpose for them (Rom. 8:28).
I cannot be separated from God.	And I am convinced that nothing can ever separate us from God's love. Neither death nor life, neither angels nor demons, neither our fears for today nor our worries about tomorrow—not even the powers of hell can separate us from God's love. No power in the sky above or in the earth below— indeed, nothing in all creation will ever be able to separate us from the love of God that is revealed in Christ Jesus our Lord (Rom. 8:38–39).
I know God is working in me.	And I am certain that God, who began the good work within you, will continue his work until it is finally finished on the day when Christ Jesus returns (Phil. 1:6).
I am a citizen of heaven.	But we are citizens of heaven, where the Lord Jesus Christ lives. And we are eagerly waiting for him to return as our Savior (Phil. 3:20).

I have power, love, and self-control.	For God has not given us a spirit of fear and timidity, but of power, love, and self-discipline (2 Tim. 1:7).
The evil one can't touch me.	I am born of God and the evil one cannot touch me. We know that God's children do not make a practice of sinning, for God's Son holds them securely, and the evil one cannot touch them (1 John 5:18).

I Am Important

I am the salt and light of the earth.	You are the salt of the earth. But what good is salt if it has lost its flavor? Can you make it salty again? It will be thrown out and trampled underfoot as worthless. You are the light of the world—like a city on a hilltop that cannot be hidden (Matt. 5:13–14).
I am a branch of the true vine.	I am the true grapevine, and my Father is the gardener. …Yes, I am the vine; you are the branches. Those who remain in me, and I in them, will produce much fruit. For apart from me you can do nothing (John 15:1, 5).
I have been chosen to bear fruit.	You didn't choose me. I chose you. I appointed you to go and produce lasting fruit, so that the Father will give you whatever you ask for, using my name (John 15:16).
I am a personal witness of Christ.	But you will receive power when the Holy Spirit comes upon you. And you will be my witnesses, telling people about me everywhere—in Jerusalem, throughout Judea, in Samaria, and to the ends of the earth (Acts 1:8).
I am the temple of God's Spirit.	Don't you realize that all of you together are the temple of God and that the Spirit of God lives in you? (1 Cor. 3:16).

| I am God's workmanship. | For we are God's masterpiece. He has created us anew in Christ Jesus, so we can do the good things he planned for us long ago (Eph. 2:10). |

Appendix B

REPLACING LIES WITH TRUTH

Lie: I am afraid.

Truth: For God has not given us a spirit of fear and timidity, but of power, love, and self-discipline (2 Tim. 1:7).

Lie: There is no hope.

Truth: "For I know the plans I have for you," says the LORD. "They are plans for good and not for disaster, to give you a future and a hope" (Jer. 29:11).

Lie: I am going to die.

Truth: I will not die; instead, I will live to tell what the LORD has done (Ps. 118:17).

Lie: Something bad will happen to me.

Truth: No evil will conquer you; no plague will come near your home (Ps. 91:10).

Lie: God doesn't hear me.

Truth: The LORD hears his people when they call to him for help. He rescues them from all their troubles (Ps. 34:17).

Lie: Nothing will ever change.

Truth: But forget all that—it is nothing compared to what I am going to do. For I am about to do something new. See, I have already begun! Do you not see it? I will make a pathway through the wilderness. I will create rivers in the dry wasteland (Isa. 43:18–19).

Lie: I don't have what it takes.

Truth: But you will receive power when the Holy Spirit comes upon you (Acts 1:8).

Lie: I am worthless.

Truth: The LORD your God has chosen you to be...his treasured possession (Deut. 14:2, ESV).

Lie: I am untalented.

Truth: For we are God's masterpiece. He has created us anew in Christ Jesus, so we can do the good things he planned for us long ago (Eph. 2:10).

Lie: I would be happy if...

Truth: The LORD has done great things for us, and we are filled with joy (Ps. 126:3, NIV). The joy of the LORD is your strength (Neh. 8:10, NIV).

Lie: Nothing is working out for me.

Truth: And we know that in all things God works for the good of those who love him, who have been called according to his purpose (Rom. 8:28, NIV).

Lie: God doesn't love me.

Truth: I am convinced that neither death nor life, neither angels nor demons, neither the present nor the future, nor any powers, neither height nor depth, nor anything else in all creation, will be able to separate us from the love of God that is in Christ Jesus our Lord (Rom. 8:38–39, NIV).

Lie: I feel rejected.

Truth: He chose us in him before the creation of the world (Eph. 1:4, NIV).

Lie: I am all alone.

Truth: Be strong and courageous. Do not be afraid; do not be discouraged, for the LORD your God will be with you wherever you go (Josh. 1:9, NIV).

Appendix C

DAILY DECLARATIONS

Todd's Daily Declarations

Because life can be stressful:

▶ I will not be anxious or frustrated because I am filled with the peace of the Holy Spirit. His grace will flow through me in every situation and conversation.

Because Julie is the most important person in the world to me:

▶ I will love the wife of my youth as my most treasured gift. I will honor her by the way I speak to her, listen to her, look at her. She will get my best and not my leftovers.

Because I want to love and lead my kids well:

▶ I am a good father, and I will remember that the greatest gift or investment I can make in my kids is to live a life in love with Jesus and His Word. That will be greater than any worldly gift I could ever afford to give them.

Because I want to love and lead my team well:

▶ I will lead my team with clarity, passion, and patience. I will always believe the best in them and ask great questions to better

understand. They will know that I love them
by the way I seek to understand.

Because my life influences others:

- ► I will set an example for the people following me in the words I use, the way I live,
  the way I love, by my faith in God, and by
  my purity (1 Tim. 4:12).

JULIE'S DAILY DECLARATIONS

My purpose

- ► Jesus is first in my life. I exist to serve and
  glorify Him. He is *for* me, and He wants me
  to flourish. I am disciplined, and I order my
  life to grow closer to Him.

- ► Because of the full, abundant life Jesus gave
  me, I will give my life and my leadership to
  create a place where people can find Him
  and experience the joy that comes from
  living out their purpose.

My people

- ► I love my husband. I will honor him by the
  way I look at him, talk to him, and talk to
  others about him. I will make him glad that
  he married me.

- ► I will lead and love my kids with intention-
  ality. I will find ways to connect with them

and give them courage to do more for God's kingdom than they ever thought possible.

▶ Because God's Spirit is in me, I will love people without reservation and believe the best about them. I do not have to fear rejection.

My problems

▶ I choose happiness, but I do not resist pain. I will do the hard thing and take the high road. I will press into uncomfortable situations because I know this will make me more like Jesus and produce a joy that will outlast today.

▶ My limitation is Your opportunity. Your strength is perfect, so I don't have to be.

PROMISES TO HOLD ON TO DURING TIMES OF DOUBT, FEAR, AND INSTABILITY

God's presence: This is my command—be strong and courageous! Do not be afraid or discouraged. For the LORD your God is with you wherever you go (Josh. 1:9).

God's peace: Then you will experience God's peace, which exceeds anything we can understand. His peace will guard your hearts and minds as you live in Christ Jesus (Phil. 4:7).

God's strength: But those who trust in the LORD will find new strength. They will soar high on wings like eagles. They will run and not grow weary. They will walk and not faint (Isa. 40:31).

God's provision: And this same God who takes care of me will supply all your needs from his glorious riches, which have been given to us in Christ Jesus (Phil. 4:19).

God's protection: The LORD is my light and my salvation—so why should I be afraid? The LORD is my fortress, protecting me from danger, so why should I tremble? (Ps. 27:1).

God's guidance: Trust in the LORD with all your heart; do not depend on your own understanding. Seek his will in all you do, and he will show you which path to take (Prov. 3:5–6).

God's healing: But he was pierced for our rebellion, crushed for our sins. He was beaten so we could be whole. He was whipped so we could be healed (Isa. 53:5).

God's faithfulness: Understand, therefore, that the LORD your God is indeed God. He is the faithful God who keeps his covenant for a thousand generations and lavishes his unfailing love on those who love him and obey his commands (Deut. 7:9).

God's comfort: Even when I walk through the darkest valley, I will not be afraid, for you are close beside me. Your rod and your staff protect and comfort me (Ps. 23:4).

God's unchanging nature: Jesus Christ is the same yesterday, today, and forever (Heb. 13:8).

HELPING A FRIEND KICK OUT DOUBT

1. **Listen without judgment:** Offer a safe space for your friend to share their thoughts and doubts without fear of being judged or dismissed. Create an environment where they feel comfortable discussing their doubts openly, without pressure to have everything figured out.

2. **Pray with and for them:** Lift them up in prayer, asking for strength, clarity, and peace during their time of doubt. Pray with them. Pray for them. This is a time when your faith can carry them.

3. **Share your doubt journey:** Share your own struggle with times of doubting God. Let them know you've been there yourself and what you did to come through your doubt with stronger faith.

4. **Send encouragement:** When you encourage someone, you are giving them courage to not give up. Send them an encouraging text throughout the week. Share scriptures to remind them of the truth. Your note will remind them that they are not alone.

5. **Remind them of God's faithfulness.** When a person is overcome with doubt they tend to forget the faithfulness of God. Point out the times God did answer prayers—all the times He did come through for them. Help them see God moving in their past.

6. **Be patient:** Understand that overcoming doubt is a process and offer patience as they navigate through their emotions. Simply being present and spending time with them can offer comfort and reassurance.

7. **Get them to church:** Encourage them to stay connected with a community of faith. They may not feel like going to church, so offer to pick them up, meet them there, and sit with them. Getting in an atmosphere of faith will help build their faith.

8. **Recommend resources:** Suggest books, podcasts, or sermons that address doubt and faith in a way that might resonate with them. Offer to study Scripture together. Reading and discussing passages that focus on faith and trust will help them build back what's missing.

9. **Help them find a mentor or counselor:** If appropriate, suggest they speak with someone experienced in guiding others through doubt, such as a pastor or counselor.

10. Respect their journey: Understand that their path to overcoming doubt may look different from yours, and that's OK. Give them the time they need.

NOTES

CHAPTER 1

1. "Building Blocks for Healthy Self-Esteem in Kids," HealthyChildren.org, accessed September 3, 2024, https://www.healthychildren.org/English/ages-stages/gradeschool/Pages/Helping-Your-Child-Develop-A-Healthy-Sense-of-Self-Esteem.aspx; see also "Signs of Low Self-Esteem in Children and Teens," HealthyChildren.org, accessed September 3, 2024, https://www.healthychildren.org/English/ages-stages/gradeschool/Pages/Signs-of-Low-Self-Esteem.aspx.
2. "Building Blocks for Healthy Self-Esteem in Kids," HealthyChildren.org; "Signs of Low Self-Esteem in Children and Teens," HealthyChildren.org.
3. Kevin Leman, *The Birth Order Book: Why You Are the Way You Are* (Revell, 1985).
4. Molly Smith, "The Impacts of Social Media on Youth Self-image," Loma Linda University Health, May 16, 2023, https://news.llu.edu/health-wellness/impacts-of-social-media-youth-self-image.
5. Leman, *The Birth Order Book*.
6. Leman, *The Birth Order Book*.
7. J. R. Sherman, *Rejection* (Pathway Books, 1982).

CHAPTER 2

1. Cory Stieg, "Simone Biles Withdrew from Final 'to Focus on My Mental Health'—Here's How to Tell If You Need a Break," CNBC LLC, July 27, 2021, https://www.cnbc.com/make-it/health-and-wellness/.
2. Craig Groeschel, *Winning the War in Your Mind* (Zondervan, 2021).
3. Caroline Leaf, *Switch On Your Brain: The Key to Peak Happiness, Thinking, and Health* (Baker Books, 2013).
4. Leaf, *Switch On Your Brain*.

5. "The Nine Enneagram Type Descriptions," The Enneagram Institute, accessed September 3, 2024, https://www.enneagraminstitute.com/type-descriptions.

CHAPTER 3

1. "Anxiety Disorders," World Health Organization, September 27, 2023, https://www.who.int/news-room/fact-sheets/detail/anxiety-disorders.
2. Michella Feldborg et al., "Perceiving the Self and Emotions with an Anxious Mind: Evidence from an Implicit Perceptual Task," *International Journal of Environmental Research and Public Health*, 18, no. 22 (2021): 12096, https://www.ncbi.nlm.nih.gov/pmc/articles/PMC8622160/.
3. Ronald C. Kessler et al., "The WHO World Mental Health (WMH) Surveys," NIH, accessed September 4, 2024, https://www.ncbi.nlm.nih.gov/pmc/articles/PMC2995950/.
4. Kessler et al., "The WHO World Mental Health (WMH) Surveys."

CHAPTER 4

1. H. Krasnova et al., "Envy on Facebook: A Hidden Threat to Users' Life Satisfaction?," *Computers in Human Behavior* 29, no. 4, (2013): 2024–2031.
2. J. Fardouly et al., "Social Comparisons on Social Media: The Impact of Instagram on Young Women's Body Image Concerns and Mood," *Cyberpsychology, Behavior, and Social Networking* 21, no. 5, (2018): 1–7.

CHAPTER 5

1. Neil P. Jones et al., "Cognitive Processes in Response to Goal Failure: A Study of Ruminative Thought and Its Affective Consequences," *Journal of Social and Clinical Psychology* vol. 32, no. 5, (2013): 482, https://www.ncbi.nlm.nih.gov/pmc/articles/PMC3864849/.

2. J. Sakulku, J. Alexander, "The Impostor Phenomenon," *International Journal of Behavioral Science* 6, no. 1 (2011): 75–76, https://so06.tci-thaijo.org/index.php/IJBS/article/view/521/pdf.

3. "Billy Graham Quotes," Goodreads, accessed September 6, 2024, https://www.goodreads.com/quotes/7481954-when-we-come-to-the-end-of-ourselves-we-come.

CHAPTER 8

1. Kevin McSpadden, "You Now Have a Shorter Attention Span Than a Goldfish," *Time*, May 1, 2015, https://time.com/3858309/attention-spans-goldfish/; see also "Average Human Attention Span Statistics and Facts [2024]," SambaRecovery, June 25, 2024, https://www.sambarecovery.com/rehab-blog/average-human-attention-span-statistics.

2. "Average Human Attention Span Statistics and Facts [2024]," SambaRecovery.

CHAPTER 9

1. "You Just Chip Away Everything That Doesn't Look Like David," Quote Investigator, June 22, 2014, https://quoteinvestigator.com/2014/06/22/chip-away/.

CHAPTER 11

1. Donald R. Hodel, "Biology of Palms and Implications for Management in the Landscape," *HortTechnology* 19, no. 4 (January 1, 2009), https://journals.ashs.org/horttech/view/journals/horttech/19/4/article-p676.xml.

2. Paul Tillich, *The Dynamics of Faith* (Harper & Row, 1957).

CHAPTER 12

1. J. M. Gottman, *The Science of Trust: Emotional Attunement for Couples* (W. W. Norton & Co., 2011).

2. E. F. Baumeister et al., "Bad Is Stronger Than Good," *Review of General Psychology* 5, no. 4 (2011), 323–370, https://psycnet.apa.org/record/2018-70020-001.

3. V. H. Murthy, "Our Epidemic of Loneliness and Isolation (2023)," Office of the US Surgeon General, accessed September 11, 2024, https://www.hhs.gov/sites/default/files/surgeon-general-social-connection-advisory.pdf.

4. Susie Demarinis, "Loneliness at Epidemic Levels in America," *Elsevier* 16, no. 5 (2020): 278–279, accessed September 11, 2024, https://www.ncbi.nlm.nih.gov/pmc/articles/PMC7321652/.

CHAPTER 13

1. Howard J. Markman et al., "The Premarital Communication Roots of Marital Distress and Divorce: The First Five Years of Marriage," *Journal of Family Psychology* 24, no. 3 (2010): 289–298, https://www.ncbi.nlm.nih.gov/pmc/articles/PMC4298140/.

2. Frank D. Fincham and Steven R. H. Beach, "Marriage in the New Millennium: A Decade in Review," *Journal of Marriage and Family* (June 18, 2010), https://onlinelibrary.wiley.com/doi/abs/10.1111/j.1741-3737.2010.00722.x.

CHAPTER 14

1. S. L. Murray, J. G. Holmes, and D. W. Griffin, "The Benefits of Positive Illusions: Idealization and the Construction of Satisfaction in Close Relationships," *Journal of Personality and Social Psychology* 70, no. 1 (1996): 79–98, https://doi.org/10.1037/0022-3514.70.1.79.

2. Dietrich Bonhoeffer, *Life Together* (HarperOne, 2009).

CHAPTER 15

1. Stephen M. R. Covey, *The Speed of Trust: The One Thing That Changes Everything* (Free Press, 2006).

2. J. K. Rempel, J. G. Holmes, and M. P. Zanna, "Trust in Close Relationships," *Journal of Personality and Social Psychology* 49, no. 1 (1985): 95–112.
3. C. S. Lewis, *The Four Loves* (Harcourt Brace, 1960).
4. Covey, *The Speed of Trust.*
5. C. S. Lewis, "On Forgiveness," in *The Weight of Glory* (Eerdmans, 1965).
6. Candace Kumai, *Kintsugi Wellness: The Japanese Art of Nourishing Mind, Body, and Spirit* (HarperCollins, 2018).

ABOUT THE AUTHOR

TODD MULLINS IS the senior pastor of Christ Fellowship Church, a vibrant, multisite congregation dedicated to transforming lives through the power of Jesus Christ. Known for his engaging teaching, Todd blends biblical truth with practical wisdom, inspiring people to live fully and boldly for Christ. He is married to his seventh-grade sweetheart, Julie. Together they have committed their lives to helping people discover the extraordinary life that God has designed for them. Todd and Julie live in South Florida, close to their adult children, Jefferson and Cassie, who serve with them in ministry. Connect with Todd and explore more of his teachings at toddmullins.org.